D1515695

YOU CHOOSE BOOKS™

The Revolutionary War Experience

An Interactive History Adventure

CAPSTONE PRESS
a capstone imprint

You Choose Books are published by Capstone Press,
1710 Roe Crest Drive, North Mankato, Minnesota 56003
www.capstonepub.com

Copyright © 2014 by Capstone Press, a Capstone imprint. All rights reserved. No part of this publication may be reproduced in whole or in part, or stored in a retrieval system, or transmitted in any form or by any means, electronic, mechanical, photocopying, recording, or otherwise, without written permission of the publisher.

Library of Congress Cataloging-in-Publication Data
Cataloging-in-publication information is on file with the Library of Congress.
ISBN 978-1-4914-1712-6 (paper over board)
ISBN 978-1-4765-2169-5 (paperback)

Photo Credits
Anne S. K. Brown Military Collection, Brown University Library, 169; Art Resource, N.Y., 138, The New York Public Library, 129; Collection of the New-York Historical Society, Uniforms of the American Revolution acc# 1921.109, 176; Corbis: Bettmann, 116, 147, 206; Courtesy of Army Art Collection, U.S. Army Center of Military History, 145; Getty Images: Archive Photos, 35, Stock Montage, 57, 70, 87, The Bridgeman Art Library/William Barnes Wollen, 107, Time Life Pictures/Mansell, 211; Library of Congress, 60, 118, 164, 174, 228, 241, 272, 318; Mary Evans Picture Library, 21, 55; National Geographic Creative: Louis S. Glanzman, 246; National Park Service: Harpers Ferry Center, 154, 180, 313, Colonial National Historical Park, 224; New York Public Library, Picture Collection: The Branch Libraries, Astor, Lenox and Tilden Foundations, 133; North Wind Picture Archives, cover (top, back, spine), 8, 14, 43, 44, 46, 65, 83, 97, 102, 122, 150, 160, 190, 195, 201, 258, 265, 278, 286, 292; *Pictorial Field Book of the Revolution* by B.J. Lossing, 1859, 236, 253, 307; Shutterstock: irisphoto1, 76, Morphart Creation, 27; The Bridgeman Art Library: National Army Museum, London, cover (bottom), 212, Private Collection, 92, Private Collection/Peter Newark American Pictures, 182; The Granger Collection, NYC, 299; www.historicalimagebank.com Painting by Don Troiani, 230, 255

Printed in China.
022014 008021

Table of Contents

The Boston Massacre:

An Interactive History Adventure

By Elizabeth Raum

Consultant:
Len Travers
Associate Professor of History
University of Massachusetts at Dartmouth

TABLE OF CONTENTS

About Your Adventure

YOU are in Boston, Massachusetts, in 1770. For months, American colonists and British soldiers have been clashing in the city. Which side will you take?

In this book you'll explore how the choices people made meant the difference between life and death. The events you'll experience happened to real people.

Chapter One sets the scene. Then you choose which path to read. Follow the directions at the bottom of each page. The choices you make will change your outcome. After you finish one path, go back and read the others for new perspectives and more adventures.

YOU CHOOSE the path you take through history.

In late 1768, British soldiers in red coats marched through the streets of Boston.

CHAPTER 1

Trouble in Boston

It's February 1770. The Province of Massachusetts and 12 other colonies in North America are under the rule of Great Britain. People in the colonies still consider themselves British. But many of them are tired of paying high prices for goods imported from Britain. They're also unhappy with the taxes they have to pay to the British government.

In 1765, the British parliament passed the Stamp Act. This law put a tax on every document, newspaper, and pamphlet printed in the colonies.

Turn the page.

In Boston, Massachusetts, a group of shopkeepers and craftsmen organized to fight the Stamp Act. They called themselves the Loyal Nine. The Loyal Nine convinced Bostonians to gather in the streets to protest the tax. The violent protests were enough to make Parliament repeal the tax in 1766.

Later, the Loyal Nine changed their name to the Sons of Liberty. Their members included silversmith Paul Revere, politician and writer Samuel Adams, and shipowner John Hancock. The group met under the Liberty Tree. This giant elm was about a block east of Boston Common park. The Sons of Liberty told Bostonians not to do business with merchants who traded with the British.

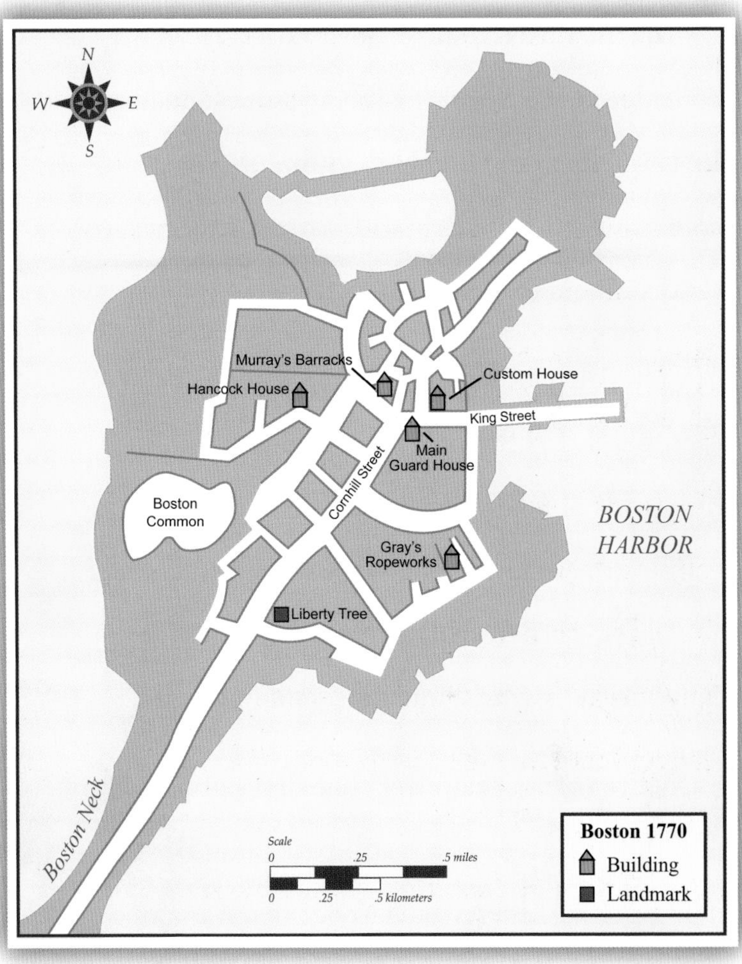
N
W
E
S
Murray's Barracks
Hancock House
Custom House
King Street
Main Guard House
Cornhill Street
Boston Common
BOSTON HARBOR
Gray's Ropeworks
Liberty Tree
Boston Neck
Scale
0
.25
.5 miles
0
.25
.5 kilometers
Boston 1770
Building
Landmark

Turn the page.

Massachusetts Governor Francis Bernard considered the Sons of Liberty troublemakers. In 1768, he asked General Thomas Gage, commander of the British Army in America, to send soldiers to Boston.

The 14th and 29th regiments arrived October 1, 1768. Soon after they arrived, hundreds of soldiers paraded through the cobblestone streets. They wore bright red coats and three-cornered black hats. At their sides, they carried swords, muskets, and bayonets.

More than a year after that first parade, about 4,000 British troops are still patrolling Boston. The Sons of Liberty haven't yet taken major action against them. But tensions are building, and Boston is in the midst of trouble.

To be a 13-year-old apprentice in Boston,
turn to page **15**.

To serve as a British soldier in Boston,
turn to page **47**.

To experience the events as John Hancock's maid,
turn to page **71**.

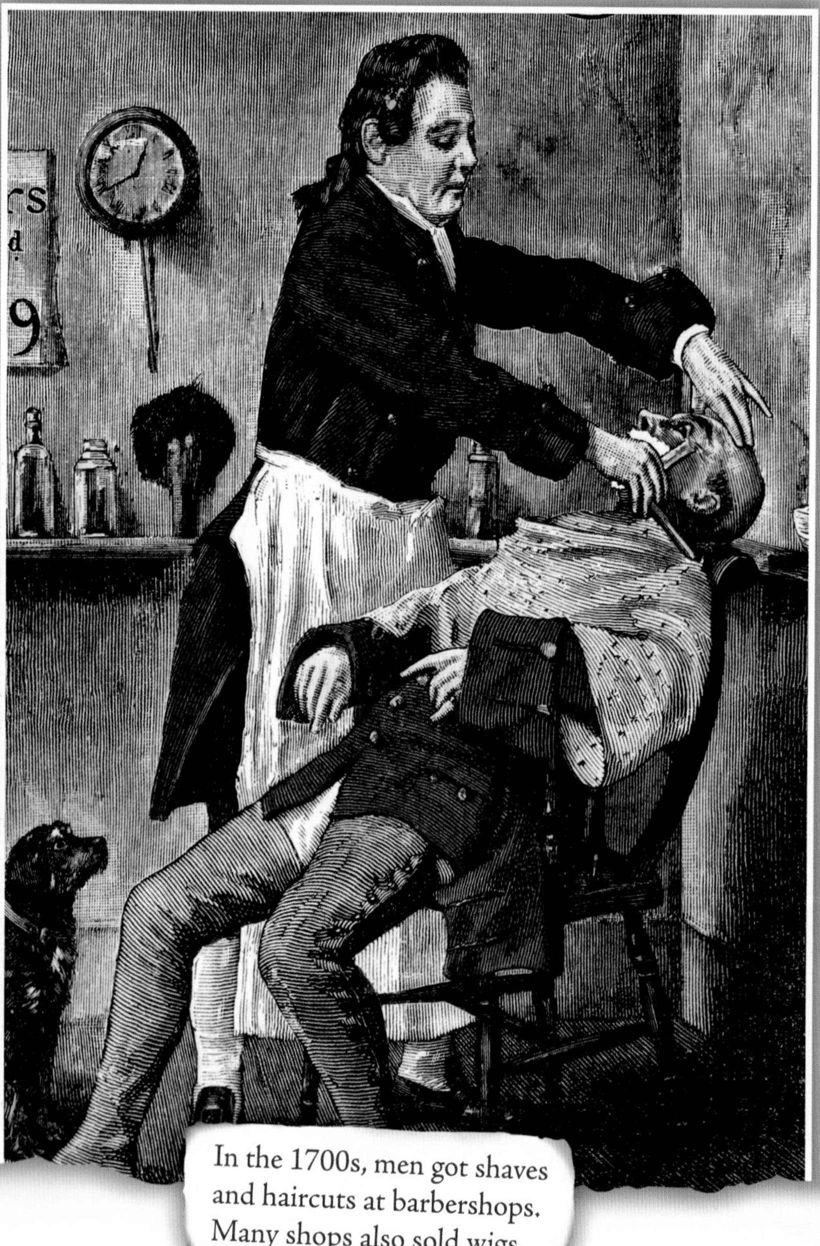

In the 1700s, men got shaves and haircuts at barbershops. Many shops also sold wigs.

CHAPTER 2

The Wigmaker's Apprentice

You roll the measuring tape into a neat coil, put the curling irons away, and sweep the powdery floor. Mr. John Piemont insists that his barbershop be kept neat and in order. At 13, you are the youngest and newest apprentice, so the job falls to you.

As an apprentice, you also make deliveries. One day, Mr. Piemont asks you to deliver a wig to Mrs. Grizzell Apthorp's house. You get hopelessly lost. You've lived in Boston only three months. With nearly 16,000 people, Boston is much bigger than the town of Framingham, where you grew up.

Turn the page.

"Are you lost?" a boy asks you.

"I'm afraid so," you reply. "I'm looking for Mrs. Apthorp's house."

He laughs. "Come with me. I work for the lady. My name's Christopher Seider."

Chris is a year or two younger than you. On the way to Mrs. Apthorp's home, you become friends. "Come back whenever you have some time off. If I'm free, I'll show you around town," he says.

You deliver the wig and return to Piemont's. In quiet moments, the older apprentices tell you about a group many of them belong to. "We're called the Sons of Liberty because we fight for liberty," one apprentice says.

"Yes," another says. "If a merchant sells imported British goods, we teach him a lesson. We smear tar on his windows, destroy his garden, and mark up his signs."

It sounds like trouble to you, but you admire their spirit. One day, you wander past the Liberty Tree, a giant elm. "It's more than 120 years old," an apprentice tells you. "The Sons of Liberty meet under it. When someone gives us a hard time, we make a dummy that looks like the person. Then we hang it from a branch of the Liberty Tree with a sign around its neck."

"We call it an effigy," another apprentice adds. "It's a warning."

You feel a shiver of excitement. These boys are part of something important.

Turn the page.

Mr. Piemont gives you a few hours off on the morning of February 22. Another apprentice, John, invites you to walk with him to Boston Neck. This strip of land connects Boston to the mainland. But then you remember Christopher Seider had invited you to visit him the next time you were free.

To go with John, go to page **19**.

To meet Chris Seider, turn to page **22**.

Once you reach Boston Neck, you see an army guard on duty. John walks up to the guard and starts yelling. "Hey, lobster back!" he shouts. You and John have a good laugh as you call the guard names. But it's cold, so you soon leave.

The next day, you arrive at work to find all of the other apprentices working silently. Their faces are pale and serious. "What's wrong?" you ask.

John answers, "Yesterday, Ebenezer Richardson killed the boy who works for Mrs. Apthorp. Christopher Seider was his name."

"How did it happen?" you cry.

"A mob attacked Theophilus Lillie for importing British goods. Richardson came to his aid. He fired his musket into the crowd," another apprentice, Edward Garrick, says.

"I knew Chris," you whisper. What if you'd been there? Could you have saved him?

Samuel Adams is organizing a funeral for Chris. All of the apprentices want to go, but someone has to help in the shop.

To go the funeral, turn to page **25**.

To stay behind to work, turn to page **26**.

Christopher Seider was shot in front of Theophilus Lillie's shop.

You find Christopher hauling charcoal near Mrs. Apthorp's house. You hear people shouting from the street. "What's going on?" you ask him.

A crowd tosses rocks at a nearby house, breaking windows. Chris tells you it's Ebenezer Richardson's home. "He's a tax collector for the British. He tried to stop a Sons of Liberty protest. Now they're teaching him a lesson."

A man tosses a bat through a window. Richardson appears at one of the broken windows. He aims a musket at the crowd. "Stand off, or I'll fire," he yells.

Chris bends down to pick up a stone. "No, Chris!" you yell. But it's too late. Richardson pulls the trigger, and Chris crumples to the ground. Several men pick him up and carry him away.

To follow the men, go to page **23**.

To return to Piemont's, turn to page **24**.

You follow the men carrying Chris to a nearby house. Maybe he's not hurt too badly. Maybe he'll be fine once he rests for a bit.

No one stops you as you enter the house. The men place Chris on a bed. A doctor rushes past you. "Where's the boy?" he shouts, and you point to the bed.

The doctor bends over Chris. "It's serious," he says. "You all need to leave now."

You leave quietly. There is nothing you can do to help. You pray that Chris will recover as you head back to the barbershop.

Turn the page.

You return to Piemont's. Later that night, you're sad to hear the news that Chris died. All the apprentices are talking about the funeral that Samuel Adams is planning.

"Samuel Adams is Boston's leading patriot," Edward Garrick says. "He writes articles for the newspaper about the way Parliament is mistreating us here in the colonies." Several apprentices are going to Chris' funeral, but someone has to stay and watch the shop.

To go to the funeral, go to page **25**.

To stay at work, turn to page **26**.

The funeral is February 26. You join hundreds of other boys walking ahead of Chris' casket through the streets of Boston. After the burial, you hurry back to the shop. If you keep busy, maybe you won't think about your friend's death.

A British soldier from the 29th Regiment, Patrick Dines, works at Piemont's shop in his spare time. You like Dines. He's a good fellow, even though he's a soldier.

After work on Monday, March 5, Dines invites several of the apprentices to visit his barracks. You're curious to see the barracks, but will going there mean you support the soldiers? Edward Garrick invites you to walk around town. "Maybe we can stir up a little trouble," he says.

To go to the barracks, turn to page **28**.

To walk around town, turn to page **29**.

You feel as if you should go to the funeral, but you're too upset. You spend the day working silently in the shop. You try not to think about Chris, but it's hard.

After the funeral, another apprentice tells you that there were at least 2,000 people there. That number included 400 schoolboys, who marched ahead of the casket.

One day in early March, several soldiers come by for shaves. When they leave, Mr. Piemont says that Captain John Goldfinch owes him money. "If you can collect it, you can keep it," he tells Edward Garrick.

It snows on Monday, March 5. By evening, the weather is clear, but the roads are still icy. "I'm off to see what's going on in the streets," Edward says. "Want to join me?"

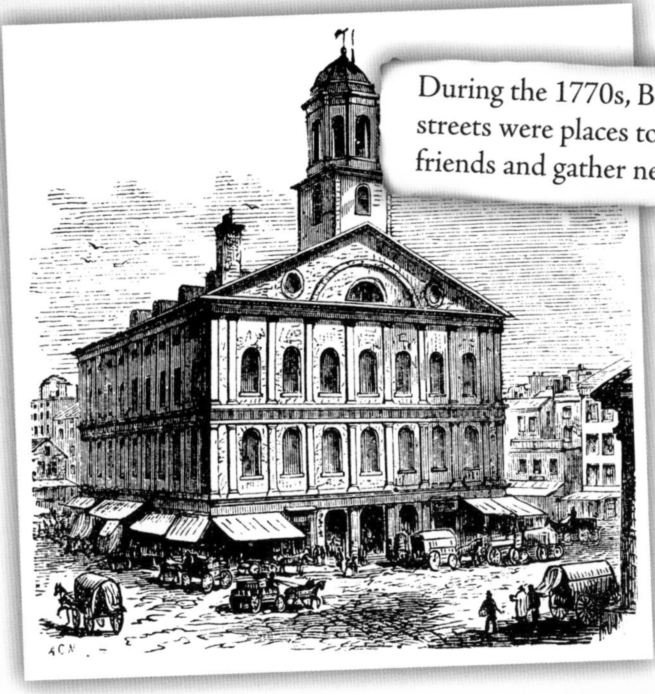

During the 1770s, Boston's streets were places to meet friends and gather news.

Just then, another apprentice, Bartholomew Broaders, comes in. He says that Mr. Green, who lives in the Custom House, asked him to walk with his daughter, Ann, and her friend. They're headed to the apothecary to pick up medicine. "Want to come with us?" Bartholomew asks you.

To go with Edward, turn to page **29.**

To go with Bartholomew, turn to page **32.**

You and two other boys go to the barracks with Dines. He shows you around as you talk to the soldiers of the 29th. You are about to leave when you overhear Sergeant Daniels say, "We've put up with the insults of these Bostonians long enough. It's time to show them who's in charge."

When you return to your lodgings, apprentice Edward Garrick says he's going out. "If there's a fight, I want to be there. You should come too."

You sneeze. Your head feels fuzzy. "I'm catching a cold. Maybe I'll stay in."

"Come with me to the apothecary," apprentice Bartholomew Broaders says. "Mr. Green, who lives in the Custom House, asked me to walk his daughter and her friend there. They'll have medicines if you feel sick."

To go with Edward, go to page **29.**

To join Bartholomew, turn to page **32.**

You and Edward walk down Cornhill Street to the Main Guard building. Across King Street, a single soldier stands at a sentry post in front of the Custom House.

While you are standing there, Captain John Goldfinch walks by. You remember that Mr. Piemont said Goldfinch owed him money. "There goes the fellow who won't pay Mr. Piemont for fixing his hair," Edward shouts. Goldfinch ignores Edward and keeps walking down the street.

Just then, Bartholomew Broaders, Ann Green, and her friend Molly Rogers arrive. They invite you and Edward inside the Custom House.

As you talk in the Custom House, you hear shouts from outside. Edward and Bartholomew want to go out and see what's going on. But you think it might be safer to stay inside.

To go outside, turn to page **30**.

To stay inside, turn to page **33**.

As you walk out of the Custom House, Edward begins complaining about Goldfinch again. The guard at the post, Private Hugh White, overhears him. "Goldfinch is a gentleman," he protests.

"There's not a gentleman in the entire regiment," Edward says.

White steps out from his post. "Let me see your face."

"I'm not ashamed to show my face," Edward says. As Edward juts out his chin, White swings his musket. It strikes Edward in the head.

"Ouch!" Edward yells in pain.

"Why did you do that?" you shout at White. "He didn't do anything to you!" You and Bartholomew pick up pebbles and pieces of ice and hurl them at White.

Suddenly, church bells begin to ring. Usually, that's a fire alarm. People begin pouring into the square to fight the fire.

"This soldier attacked my friend for no reason at all!" you shout to the growing crowd.

"Lousy rascal! Redcoat!" The crowd shouts insults and hurls rocks at White. White raises his musket. "If they attack me, I will fire," he says.

"Let's get out of here," you say to Edward.

"Go ahead if you want," he replies. "But I'm not leaving."

To stay with Edward, turn to page **34**.

To go back to your lodgings, turn to page **41**.

As you walk with Bartholomew and the girls, groups of soldiers pass you. You also see a group of club-carrying townspeople. You walk faster. When you reach the Custom House, Edward is there. You all decide to go inside.

As you talk with your friends, you hear noises from the streets outside. "Let's go see what's going on," Edward says.

"I don't think that's a good idea," you reply. "I'm staying here." Edward and Bartholomew slip out the front door.

You don't want to be in the middle of the action, but you still want to see what's happening. You and the girls walk upstairs and look out the window at the street below. There's a British soldier standing at a sentry post in front of the Custom House.

From the window, you see Edward and Bartholomew arguing with the sentry. A crowd gathers around them. Some soldiers come to help the sentry, but the crowd won't let them move.

Suddenly, you hear a gunshot. More shots follow. Several men fall into the street, bleeding. You slip back to your lodgings. There you hear that 11 men were shot, and at least three died. Edward and Bartholomew weren't hurt.

The next day, one of the Sons of Liberty asks you what happened at the Custom House. "We have a report that shots were fired from inside. It will help our cause if we have a witness who saw the soldiers firing from that location," he tells you.

You want to help, but you know soldiers weren't inside the Custom House. And you didn't see the shots being fired.

To tell the truth, turn to page **38.**

To lie, turn to page **39.**

Edward might need your help. You stay. Edward's moans stir up the crowd. They throw sticks and stones at the guard.

A mob comes up the street swinging bats and clubs. A large, dark-skinned man armed with a club leads the group. "That's Crispus Attucks," someone says. "And there's Sam Gray," another adds. "He fought with some soldiers at the ropeworks on Friday."

More people pour into King Street. Some carry buckets to fight what they believe is a fire. Others carry bats, swords, or clubs. One man rips the leg off a market stand to use as a weapon. You stand in the middle of the crowd, unsure of what to do.

Private White calls for help. "Turn out the Main Guard!"

Crispus Attucks was at the front of the Boston Massacre protesters.

Captain Thomas Preston arrives with a small group of soldiers. As they try to cross King Street, they disappear into the crowd. They finally reach White at his post.

White falls in with the other soldiers. Preston tries to march them back to the Main Guard building. But the crowd blocks them. "Fire!" the townspeople yell at the soldiers. "Fire your guns!"

You turn away, ready to run. "Don't be afraid, lad," a man says to you. "They dare not fire."

Then a gun goes off. Boom!

Turn the page.

The crowd pushes toward Royal Exchange Lane and down King Street. You have no choice but to flee with them. As you look back, you see several coats lying in the snow. Then you realize that they aren't coats. They are the bodies of the men shot by the British soldiers.

You feel sick. You've lost track of Edward and Bartholomew. Are they among the dead?

When you get back to your lodgings, the other boys are already there. You sigh with relief, but your heart is heavy. Eleven men were shot, and at least three died. Your taunts may have been partly to blame. Edward says that it was bound to happen. You only tossed pebbles and ice. The soldiers were the ones with guns.

The next day, some of the Sons of Liberty stop by the barbershop. They want to take statements from everyone who saw the shootings. You're not sure if you saw enough to give an accurate account.

To give a statement, turn to page **40.**

To refuse, turn to page **42.**

You give an honest account of the shooting. When asked if anyone shot a gun out of the windows of the Custom House, you say no. Even though others disagree, you don't change your story.

At first, you are afraid that the Sons of Liberty will call you a traitor, but that never happens. Maybe that's what freedom is about. You are free to tell the truth as you see it. You feel calm and believe the whole truth will come out in the trial.

THE END

To follow another path, turn to page 13.
To read the conclusion, turn to page 103.

You say that soldiers fired from the windows of the Custom House. After all, it's important that the soldiers are punished.

But by the end of the week, you realize that you can't live with telling a lie. You find the man who took your testimony and confess.

"The truth will come out at the trial," he says. "They probably won't even call on you to testify, but we wanted to get as many accounts as we could. Some were accurate, but there may have been others like yours — people who stretched the truth a bit to serve the cause. I thank you for being a true Son of Liberty."

You can't help but smile. You are a patriot. When you are older, you'll fight for liberty.

THE END

To follow another path, turn to page 13.
To read the conclusion, turn to page 103.

You try to give an honest account. You are certain the captain said, "Fire!" Samuel Adams writes about the shootings in the *Boston Gazette*. He calls it the Boston Massacre. Paul Revere prints an engraving that shows soldiers firing into an unarmed crowd. Maybe he was there that night, but you never saw him.

After a while, you forget what you actually saw. You are convinced that whatever happened was the soldiers' fault. They'll go to trial. Even with famous lawyers John Adams and Josiah Quincy defending them, they'll probably be found guilty. You expect to see them hanged on Boston Common.

THE END

To follow another path, turn to page 13.
To read the conclusion, turn to page 103.

You return to your lodgings and get ready for bed. But you can't fall asleep. You're worried about Edward and Bartholomew.

Several hours later, the other boys slip into the room. As Edward lights a candle, you see that his face is pale. "What happened after I left?" you ask him.

"The Redcoats fired on the crowd," Edward replies. "Eleven men were shot. Sam Gray was killed. So was Crispus Attucks. I'm not sure about the rest."

The next day, the soldiers are arrested. Once the soldiers' trials are over, you hope Boston will be peaceful again.

THE END

To follow another path, turn to page 13.
To read the conclusion, turn to page 103.

"I'd like to help," you say, "but I didn't see exactly what happened."

The men talk to other apprentices. A few days later, you meet one of the men in the street. "You're the boy who wanted to help, aren't you?" he asks.

You nod. He hands you a pile of printed handbills. "This is an engraving Paul Revere made of the Boston Massacre. You can help our cause by dropping these off at shops and handing them out all over town. We want everyone to know what happened on March 5, 1770."

As he walks away, you look at Mr. Revere's picture of British soldiers shooting into a helpless crowd. This is not what you saw. The townspeople had clubs and bats. They were throwing ice, shells, and dirt. Should you help distribute a picture that you know isn't accurate?

Paul Revere made an engraving of the Boston Massacre, based on a drawing by Henry Pelham.

To distribute the handbills, turn to page **44.**

To toss them, turn to page **45.**

You distribute the handbills. A picture like this is bound to convince people that the British soldiers must leave the colonies. Does it really matter whether or not the picture is accurate?

Paul Revere and other patriots distributed handbills showing his engraving of the massacre.

THE END

To follow another path, turn to page 13.
To read the conclusion, turn to page 103.

You hide the handbills under your coat and return to work. Later, you slip the bills under a loose floorboard. No one will ever know that you didn't distribute them. People believe what they see on paper, even if it's wrong. You'll find better ways to help the cause of liberty.

THE END

To follow another path, turn to page 13.
To read the conclusion, turn to page 103.

Boston schoolboys sometimes taunted and threw things at the British soldiers.

CHAPTER 3

A King's Soldier in Boston

"Redcoat!" a young boy yells. "Bloodyback!" Another boy hurls a rock along with his insults.

You duck just in time. In the last few months, people have tossed stones, dirt, ice, and snowballs at you as you walk the streets of Boston.

You'd like to knock some sense into the boys, but you can't. You're a soldier in the king's army. Your job is to protect the people of Boston. It wouldn't be right to strike out at them, even though they deserve it.

Turn the page.

Some of your fellow soldiers are letting the tension get to them. One had too much to drink one night and rode his horse into a family's parlor. Instead of being embarrassed, the soldier just laughed and rode back outside.

Some soldiers hold target practice outside churches on Sunday mornings to disturb the people inside. Others tease ladies on their way to market or steal apples from farmers' carts. It seems childish to you, but you understand why they've decided to fight back. You're all tired of being the enemy. When you see farmers coming to town on market day, you think about what a good life they must have.

One November day in 1769, you go to Piemont's Barbershop for a shave. As you leave the shop, a man comes up to you. You've seen him before. He's always been friendly and respectful.

"May I have a word, sir?" he asks. When you agree, he pulls you into a side alley.

"I have an opportunity for you," he says. "There are some of us here in Boston who know you are not the enemy. Have you given any thought to staying here in the colonies?" He offers to help you settle in America if you'll desert the British Army.

You're tempted. There's nothing for you in Britain. Your family is poor, and the life of a soldier is hard. The army pays very little. If you stay, you might be able to become a farmer. But you'll be a deserter. The army hangs deserters. "We'll protect you," the man says. Can he?

To stay in the army, turn to page **50**.

To desert, turn to page **52**.

You say no to the man's offer. Deserters deserve to hang. You do wish the army paid better, though. To earn extra money, you take a job unloading cargo from ships in the harbor.

You are in the barracks on the afternoon of Friday, March 2, 1770. Patrick Walker returns from Gray's Ropeworks. His face is red with anger. "What happened?" you ask.

"I was looking for work," he says. "But instead, I was insulted and knocked down, just because I'm a soldier. Go back to the ropeworks with me. We'll get even."

You, Walker, and eight or nine other soldiers arrive at the ropeworks ready to fight. But in the meantime, the ropeworkers called for their friends, who showed up with clubs. You don't stand a chance against so many. You return to the barracks to get more soldiers.

Once you are back at the barracks, you have second thoughts. What's the point of making the brawl worse? Maybe you'll go to the tavern instead. The owner's wife cooks a fine stew. Just thinking about it makes you hungry.

To go to the tavern, turn to page 53.

To join the fight, turn to page 54.

"Yes," you say. "I'll accept your offer and leave the army."

"Then it's settled. We can hide you here in Boston. You're one of us now."

But there's another choice. The man offers you the chance to go to Rhode Island. "There's a wealthy man there, a friend of liberty, who will give you a small plot of land to farm."

To stay in Boston, turn to page **58**.

To move to Rhode Island, turn to page **64**.

You have supper at the tavern and then return to your barracks. Several bruised soldiers stagger back from the ropeworks. It's clear that the ropeworkers won this round.

On the evening of Monday, March 5, you plan to return to the tavern. But several soldiers ask you to join them in a walk around town. "Trouble's brewing. We plan to show the townspeople who's in charge."

It sounds like another foolish fight. But at some point you'll have to deal with these rebellious Bostonians.

To go to the tavern, turn to page **56**.

To join the soldiers, turn to page **59**.

At the ropeworks, you fight with a mob of ropeworkers and others who work in the area. There are too many of them for you to win the fight. After returning to the barracks to ask more soldiers to help, you try again. But once again, the workers have the upper hand.

On Saturday, three of your fellow soldiers go back to the ropeworks. During the fight that follows, Private John Rodgers suffers a broken arm and a cracked skull. This news makes you even angrier. But you won't be able to do anything about it tomorrow. Sunday is for attending church services, not fighting.

"Wait until Monday night," a soldier says. "We'll settle this once and for all."

"I wish I could go with you," you say, but you have guard duty that evening. Your shift follows that of Private Hugh White.

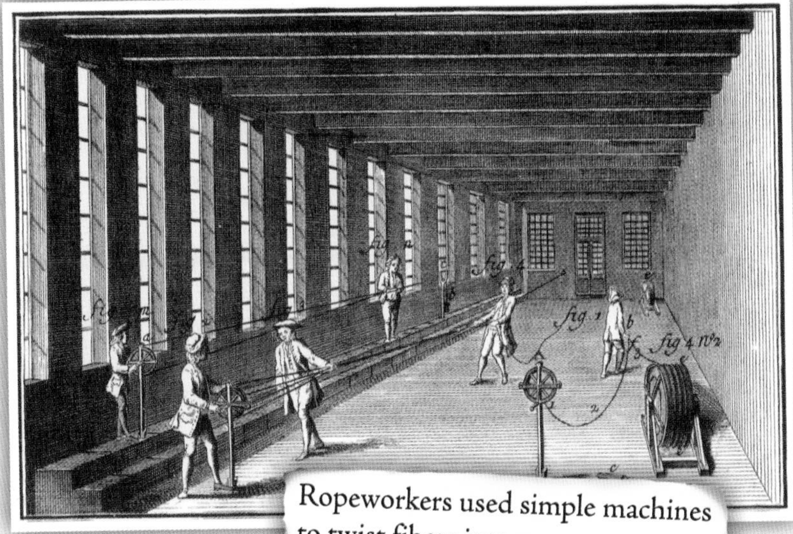

Ropeworkers used simple machines to twist fibers into rope.

On Monday night, you are polishing your musket in the barracks. You hear White shout, "Turn out, Main Guard!" Church bells begin clanging. That usually means there's a fire.

"Turn out, Main Guard!" White calls again.

Captain Thomas Preston shouts, "I need men to help White at the sentry post."

To volunteer to help White, turn to page **61**.

To wait, turn to page **66**.

You go to the tavern and notice groups of soldiers and townspeople in the streets. Church bells begin to ring. Is it a fire alarm? People rush from houses carrying buckets. You run out into the street.

"Where's the fire?" you ask a man.

"There's no fire. It's a riot."

In front of the Custom House, five or six soldiers stand in a semicircle, holding their guns. A crowd yells insults and tosses rocks and pieces of ice at the soldiers. You circle behind the crowd toward your barracks.

Someone yells, "Fire!"

Boom! A shot rings out.

You run toward the barracks. An armed soldier brushes past you, kneels down, and points his gun at the townspeople.

In the confusion, no one was sure who gave the order to shoot.

"Stop," an officer yells at him. "Don't shoot!"

The soldier doesn't put down his musket. The officer turns to you. "Take away his gun!" he yells at you.

"Don't touch me!" the soldier with the musket says. He swings his gun in your direction.

To stop the soldier, turn to page **68**.

To leave him alone, turn to page **69**.

"I'll stay in Boston," you say. You leave your barracks one day and never return. For several weeks, you live in a shopkeeper's attic. The shopkeeper is a member of the Sons of Liberty.

After a month of hiding, you take a job on a fishing boat. One day on shore, you notice a man watching you. The man looks familiar. He's not in uniform. Is he from your former regiment?

That night, you mention the stranger to the shopkeeper. "He could be an army agent," he says. "Maybe you should leave. We have friends in Rhode Island who would gladly take you in."

You like Boston and working on the fishing boat. Most of the time, the boat is out to sea. You're safe then. But are you safe enough?

To go to Rhode Island, turn to page **64**.

To stay in Boston, turn to page **67**.

You join a group of soldiers walking through Draper's Alley to Cornhill Street and onto Brattle Street. A large crowd of townspeople with clubs and sticks pound on buildings along the streets and alleyways. They are noisy, but you don't think they are dangerous.

But when you return to the barracks, a mob is waiting. People in the crowd throw snow, ice, and oyster shells at you. You cover your head as officers hustle you and the other soldiers inside.

Later that night, you hear that the soldiers shot 11 civilians in front of the Custom House. Three died at the scene. "They've arrested Captain Preston and eight soldiers," an officer tells you.

"They would never shoot into an unarmed crowd," you say.

Turn the page.

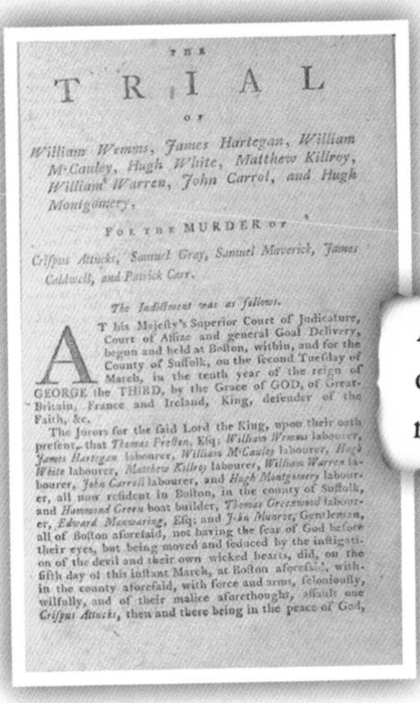

THE

TRIAL

OF

William Wemms, James Hartegan, William M'Cauley, Hugh White, Matthew Killroy, William Warren, John Carrol, and Hugh Montgomery,

FOR THE MURDER OF

Crispus Attucks, Samuel Gray, Samuel Maverick, James Caldwell, and Patrick Carr.

The Indictment was as follows.

AT his Majesty's Superior Court of Judicature, Court of Assize and general Goal Delivery, begun and held at Boston, within, and for the County of Suffolk, on the second Tuesday of March, in the tenth year of the reign of GEORGE the THIRD, by the Grace of GOD, of Great-Britain, France and Ireland, King, defender of the Faith, &c.

The Jurors for the said Lord the King, upon their oath present, that *Thomas Preston*, Esq; *William Wemms* labourer, *James Hartegan* labourer, *William M'Cauley* labourer, *Hugh White* labourer, *Matthew Killroy* labourer, *William Warren* labourer, *John Carroll* labourer, and *Hugh Montgomery* labourer, all now resident in Boston, in the county of Suffolk, and *Hammond Green* boat builder, *Thomas Greenwood* labourer, *Edward Manwaring*, Esq; and *John Munroe*, Gentleman, all of Boston aforesaid, not having the fear of God before their eyes, but being moved and seduced by the instigation of the devil and their own wicked hearts, did, on the fifth day of this instant March, at Boston aforesaid, within the county aforesaid, with force and arms, feloniously, wilfully, and of their malice aforethought, assault one *Crispus Attucks*, then and there being in the peace of God,

A poster listed the names of the soldiers tried for the murders of the civilians.

"The crowd was armed, all right — with clubs, sticks, and swords," the officer says. "But since they didn't have guns, there will be a trial. I doubt it will be fair."

You nod, relieved that you didn't have to face the crowd. Maybe now you'll be sent home. You've seen enough of America to last a lifetime.

THE END

To follow another path, turn to page 13.
To read the conclusion, turn to page 103.

You are one of six privates who go to White's aid. Captain Preston and Corporal William Wemms march beside you. You carry a musket. It's unloaded, but it has a fixed bayonet. When the crowd begins pushing, you use the bayonet to lightly jab anyone who gets too close.

You load your musket when you reach the sentry box. Preston orders White to join your formation. Preston then orders all of you to march back to the Main Guard.

But the crowd presses too close. You can't move. You form a semicircle as you stand a body-width apart from one another. Preston is in front of you. "Go home," he yells to the crowd.

People pelt him with snowballs and insults. "Fire!" the crowd yells. "Fire your guns!"

Turn the page.

It's a dare. Your finger itches to pull the trigger, but Preston told you not to fire. You tremble, both in anger and fear.

Someone throws a club at Private Hugh Montgomery, knocking him down. Boom! Private Montgomery's gun goes off.

"Fire!" someone yells. Is it Preston? It must be.

You shoot into the crowd. More shots roar from the muskets of the other soldiers.

"Stop firing!" It's Captain Preston. You put down your gun.

When the crowd clears, you see bodies in the street. Four? Five?

"What have we done?" you whisper in horror. Men are dead. Were they armed? Did they fire?

Preston marches you back to the Main Guard. He calls out the entire guard and positions groups of soldiers along King Street. You are prepared for another attack. But it never comes. The crowd leaves, and you return to the barracks.

You can't sleep. You are still awake at 2:00 in the morning when Sheriff Stephen Greenleaf comes to arrest Captain Preston.

Early that morning, you and the other seven soldiers turn yourselves in to the authorities. You shiver in your jail cell. There will be a trial. If you're found guilty, you could be sentenced to die. You hope that the colonists will treat you fairly and set you free.

THE END

To follow another path, turn to page 13.
To read the conclusion, turn to page 103.

You take the offer to move to Tiverton, Rhode Island. At first, you help the landowner farm his land. In time, the town gives you your own piece of land. You join the local Sons of Liberty.

In March 1770, you hear bad news from Boston. A dispute between British soldiers and townspeople ended with 11 colonists being shot. Five of them died. You're glad you left Boston and weren't involved.

In April 1775, the Revolutionary War begins between Great Britain and the colonists. You help the patriot cause as a drill leader of the local militia. These soldiers will be aiming their guns at men who used to be your countrymen. You hope that the fight ends quickly without too many losses on either side.

Members of colonial militias fought against British soldiers during the Revolutionary War.

THE END

To follow another path, turn to page 13.
To read the conclusion, turn to page 103.

You remain in the barracks. You hear the angry shouts of the mob, followed by musket blasts. Later that night, one of the men who had gone with Preston says, "We had no choice. If we hadn't shot into the crowd, they would have killed us."

Captain Preston is arrested very early the next morning. A few hours later, the eight soldiers who were with him turn themselves in to the authorities. Within a few days, the rest of the soldiers in Boston are moved to Castle William. This fort is on Castle Island, 3 miles from shore in Boston Harbor. By the time the trials begin, you are off on another mission for the king.

THE END

To follow another path, turn to page 13.
To read the conclusion, turn to page 103.

A few days later, as you eat supper with the shopkeeper and his family, the door bursts open. You're horrified to see a British Army captain and several soldiers standing there.

The man you saw at the docks was a British agent. He reported you to the army commander.

"You are under arrest for desertion," the captain roars.

Soldiers drag you off to the barracks. Two days later, they march you to Boston Common. You die with a noose around your neck.

THE END

To follow another path, turn to page 13.
To read the conclusion, turn to page 103.

You knock the soldier's gun aside before he can fire. You and the officer grab the soldier and push him inside the barracks.

The next day, you hear soldiers shot 11 townspeople in front of the Custom House. Three of them died at the scene. Nine soldiers are arrested and will be tried for murder.

A few days later, you are shipped to Castle William, a fort on an island in Boston Harbor. From there, you are sent back to Great Britain. There, you wait for news of the soldiers' trials. You hope that their lives will be spared.

THE END

To follow another path, turn to page 13.
To read the conclusion, turn to page 103.

You stand aside. The soldier raises his gun. Before he can fire, the officer knocks him over from behind. "Help me get him inside," the officer tells you.

You take one of the man's arms while the officer takes the other. You march the soldier to the barracks.

Later that night, you hear that the soldiers in front of the Custom House did fire on the crowd. Eleven men were shot, and three died at the scene. The nine soldiers accused of shooting them will be tried for murder.

A few days later, your regiment leaves Boston. You say a silent goodbye to your fellow soldiers in prison. You hope they will get fair trials.

THE END

To follow another path, turn to page 13.
To read the conclusion, turn to page 103.

John Hancock was one
of Boston's most famous
merchants and patriots.

CHAPTER 4

The Maid's Story

You wake before sunrise. It's hard to get out of bed on these cold February mornings. But it's your job to light the fires. First, you light the kitchen fireplace. Then you tiptoe throughout Mr. John Hancock's big house. You stir the embers in each fireplace and add wood so that the house will be toasty by daybreak.

Mr. Hancock's house sits high atop Beacon Hill, surrounded by elegant gardens. After all, Mr. Hancock is one of Boston's leaders. His ships carry goods all around the world.

Turn the page.

"You'll be amazed who comes here to meet with Mr. Hancock," Cook said when you came to work at the big house. "Many of the leaders of the Sons of Liberty — Paul Revere, Samuel Adams, and Will Molineux. Remember, what happens in this house stays in this house. Don't wag your tongue in the streets of Boston. If you can't keep a secret, you don't belong here."

Now that you've been here several months, Cook trusts you. She lumbers into the kitchen and puts on a pot of water to boil. "We're nearly out of Labrador tea," she says. "Oh, how I miss real English tea."

There's been no real tea for some time now. The Sons of Liberty won't allow it, because tea is imported from Britain. Labrador tea is made from a bush. It's a poor substitute for real tea, but Cook would never disobey Mr. Hancock.

"After you get the tea, go to Mr. Revere's shop. He's made a fine silver bowl for Mr. Hancock."

Cook warns you to be careful. Newspapers tell of British soldiers bothering girls and women, beating up boys, and causing all sorts of trouble.

You stop to watch the cows grazing on Boston Common. They remind you of your home, a farm near Lexington, Massachusetts. Today, February 22, is your brother's birthday. Even though you enjoy life in the big city, you miss your family.

There's a commotion in the street near Mr. Revere's shop. One of his apprentices rushes past. "Come quick," he says. "It's Mr. Theophilus Lillie. He imports and sells goods from Britain. Some of the boys plan to teach him a lesson."

To join the crowd, turn to page 74.

To pick up the bowl and go home, turn to page 76.

You dash after the apprentice. The street is filled with people. They are blocking the entrance to Mr. Lillie's shop. The windows of the shop are covered with tar and feathers. Several schoolboys are hurling rocks at the shop. A sign on a post has a hand pointing to Lillie's shop. Below the hand is the word "importer."

A man in a wagon tries to knock down the sign. As the man jumps from the wagon and runs down the street, the boys follow him. They throw clumps of dirt, sticks, and stones at him before he disappears into his house.

"That's Ebenezer Richardson," the apprentice tells you. "He's a tax collector."

A man tosses a bat through Richardson's window. "Ouch!" cries a woman inside. The boys continue to throw rocks. Then Richardson appears at one of the broken windows.

"Stand off or I'll fire," Richardson yells. He points a musket at the crowd. One look at his face tells you that he is serious. You know you should slip through a back alley to safety. But you want to see what will happen next.

To stay, turn to page 78.

To slip away, turn to page 82.

Paul Revere was featured on a 1954 U.S. postage stamp.

There's enough trouble in Boston without looking for more. You stop at Revere's shop to pick up the bowl and then head home.

You are in the kitchen helping Cook when one of the stablehands rushes into the house. "There was a shooting in front of Ebenezer Richardson's house," he says. "A boy was shot. He'll likely die."

"A boy?" Cook says, wringing her hands. "Samuel Adams said that all Boston needs is a spark, and it will explode in violence." Is this the spark?

The next day, you learn that Richardson wounded two men and killed 11-year-old Christopher Seider. "They are planning a big funeral, starting near the Liberty Tree," Cook says. "You can go if you want, but I'll stay here and watch the house. With these soldiers running wild, I'm afraid they might damage Mr. Hancock's property."

To go to the funeral, turn to page **85**.

To watch the house, turn to page **88**.

You stay to see what happens.

Richardson fires into the crowd. A young boy standing beside you tumbles forward. Blood oozes from his chest and stomach. He's just a boy, only 11 or 12 years old. How could such a thing happen?

You reach out to help him, but several men rush forward, lift the boy, and carry him home. Maybe you could help.

To follow the men, go to page **79**.

To return to Mr. Hancock's house, turn to page **81**.

The men carry the boy to a nearby house. You are about to go in when a doctor rushes past you. "Where is the boy?" he shouts as he disappears into the dark house.

"Who are you?" a woman at the door asks.

"I saw what happened," you stammer. "I thought maybe I could help."

"You'd best be going along now. The doctor will take charge. Christopher is in no condition to see anyone."

You don't say a word about the shooting to Cook when you return. You enjoy running errands. If Cook thought you were in danger, she'd never let you out again.

Turn the page.

The next morning, Cook says, "Mr. Hancock says Ebenezer Richardson shot and killed a boy yesterday. He wounded two men as well."

"The boy died?" you gasp.

"What's wrong?" Cook asks. "You're as pale as a peeled potato."

"He was standing beside me," you say. "He was as close as you are."

Cook puts an arm around your shoulders. "These are bad times," she says. "We have to be extra careful now. Mr. Hancock says there's to be a big funeral for the boy. You should go. It helps to mourn."

"You're right," you reply. "I'll go to the funeral and pay my respects."

Turn to page **85**.

You flee to the safety of Mr. Hancock's house and tell no one what you have seen. You're afraid that Cook will send someone else on errands if she finds out the truth.

Cook tells you later that the boy, Christopher Seider, died. The Sons of Liberty are organizing a huge funeral for Monday afternoon, February 26. Mr. Hancock encourages everyone in his household to go. But a few must stay to watch the house. Cook fears that the soldiers will cause trouble.

To go to the funeral, turn to page **85**.

To stay home, turn to page **88**.

You turn and dash into the alley. You are almost into the next street when the bell of the New Brick Church on Hanover Street begins to toll. A crowd surges through the alley, forcing you back toward Richardson's house. You watch as men grab Richardson.

"What happened?" you ask.

"Richardson fired into the crowd, wounding two men and a boy. The boy's badly hurt. They say he's dying."

A man appears with a noose. He ties it on a signpost. "Hang him," the crowd calls.

"Stop!" Will Molineux steps forward. "You can't take justice into your own hands!" he shouts to the crowd. "Take Richardson to a judge and make sure he has a proper trial."

John Hancock's elegant house was located in the Beacon Hill neighborhood.

Reluctantly, the men agree. As the mob drags Richardson off in one direction, you head back to Mr. Hancock's house. You're relieved. You didn't want to witness a hanging.

Turn the page.

In the *Boston Gazette,* Samuel Adams reports that 11-year-old Christopher Seider was the victim of Richardson's gunfire. He organizes a funeral for Seider and invites all "friends of liberty" to attend.

You consider yourself a friend of liberty, so you plan to go. But Cook asks you to stay and help guard the house. She worries that soldiers will destroy Mr. Hancock's property if no one is home.

To go to the funeral, go to page **85.**

To stay home, turn to page **88.**

You've never seen such a big funeral parade. It begins at the Seider home just beyond the Liberty Tree. About 2,000 people attend the funeral service. At least 400 schoolboys walk ahead of the casket.

Friday, March 2, is your day off. Your friend Sarah invites you to go for a walk.

"Let's go down to the South End to Mr. John Gray's Ropeworks," Sarah says. "I want you to meet my boyfriend, Sam Gray. He works there."

Boston has several ropeworks. These places make and repair the ropes used on ships. You and Sarah walk down Pearl Street and reach the ropeworks just as a British soldier marches in.

Turn the page.

The soldier asks for a job. It's not unusual for soldiers to look for work in town. They are always short of money.

"You can clean the outhouse," one of the ropeworkers yells at the soldier.

The soldier's face turns as red as his coat. "Clean it yourself!" he yells back. The shouting match soon turns into a fist fight, but the soldier is outnumbered when the other workers join in.

"You'll be sorry you insulted me," the soldier says as he runs out the door. "I'll be back, and I won't be alone."

Sam walks over to say hello. "Nice to meet you," he says to you. "But you both should leave. It's too dangerous here."

Soldiers and townspeople clashed in the days before the Boston Massacre.

You think that Sam's probably right. But Sarah's not worried. She wants to stay.

To leave, turn to page **90**.

To stay, turn to page **91**.

Cook is pleased that you've decided to stay and help her watch the house. You are both in the kitchen having a cup of Labrador tea when a message arrives for you from your father: "Mother is very ill. Come home."

You know right away that you must go. Your mother is expecting a baby soon. You hope that she'll be all right.

You borrow one of Mr. Hancock's horses. By the time you reach Lexington, Mother is dying. She had a difficult time giving birth to your baby sister.

You bend down to speak with Mother. She takes your hand and whispers, "Promise me you'll take care of the baby."

"Yes, of course." You'd promise anything if it would help. But nothing you can say or do saves her life. She slips from sleep to death later that afternoon.

After her simple funeral, you tell your father, "I promised Mother I'd take care of baby Jane."

"Then go back to Boston," he says. You understand what he means. Your 12-year-old sister Molly can watch the baby, but she can't earn money to help support the family. You've been sending your pay home, and you know the family needs it. But what about the promise you made to your mother?

To return to Boston, turn to page **92**.

To stay in Lexington, turn to page **96**.

"We should go," you tell Sarah. A few minutes later, the soldier returns with several other soldiers. Ropeworkers armed with clubs are there to meet them.

"You don't want to get in the middle of this," Sam tells Sarah. You and Sarah leave the ropeworks just as the fight begins.

When Sarah stops by on Sunday night, she tells you that the fighting isn't over. "The soldiers came back for another fight on Saturday. Sam says we'll get even one way or the other. Tomorrow night, if the church bells ring, it will mean trouble."

Monday night around 9:00, the church bells do begin to ring.

To run outside, turn to page **93**.

To stay inside, turn to page **99**.

As you walk out the door, the soldier returns with several of his friends. You and Sarah duck into the alley. "At least we can see them without being in the middle of the fight," you say. The ropeworkers use clubs to hold off the soldiers. But as the soldiers leave, they yell that they'll be back.

You return to work at Mr. Hancock's. It's a tense weekend in Boston. Soldiers interrupt church services. Everyone seems nervous.

Around 9:00 on Monday night, March 5, the church bells begin to ring. "It's a fire!" Cook yells.

You grab a bucket to help fight the fire. But Cook holds you back. "What if it's not a fire? I have a bad feeling. I think you should stay inside."

To run outside, turn to page **93**.

To stay inside, turn to page **99**.

In a shipbuilding city like Boston, much activity centered around the wharf and harbor.

Your brother, Thomas, returns to Boston with you. He hopes to find a job there too. You reach Mr. Hancock's house on Monday, March 5. Thomas heads to the wharf to look for a job.

By nightfall, Thomas still hasn't returned. You worry that he's become lost. At 9:00, the church bells ring. That usually means a fire. Normally, you would go help fight the fire. But maybe you should wait in case Thomas returns.

To go outside, turn to page **100**.

To wait at the house, turn to page **101**.

You race outside. A large crowd is gathered in the street. You follow the crowd to King Street. Everyone is yelling and shouting. Young boys are throwing pebbles and snowballs at the soldiers. "Stand off!" the soldiers yell.

People in the crowd are taunting the soldiers. "Fire!" they yell. "Fire your guns!"

Boom!

A man near you cries out. Edward Payne, standing in the entry door of his shop, grabs his arm. "I've been shot."

You help him inside, where his wife binds the wound to stop the bleeding. "Please find a doctor," she begs.

Turn the page.

You dash outside to find the doctor. People are yelling, shouting, and pushing one another. Church bells clang. The streets are dangerous. You should get back to Mr. Hancock's house as quickly as possible. But Mr. Payne needs help.

To return home, go to page **95**.

To run for the doctor, turn to page **98**.

You turn and run as fast as you can toward Mr. Hancock's house. You feel bad about not getting the doctor for Mr. Payne. But with people being shot in the streets, you could be next.

You're panting by the time you reach Mr. Hancock's door. As you slip inside, Cook is there to meet you.

Turn to page **99**.

"But I promised Mother that I'd stay and look after the baby," you say.

Your father doesn't say anything for a minute. You know he's thinking about Mother. "Well, maybe you're right," he finally says. "Caring for a baby is too much for Molly. There's plenty of chores to keep both of you busy."

You are shopping in Lexington when you hear about the Boston Massacre. On March 5, a group of British soldiers fired into a crowd of townspeople. Eleven men were shot, and five of them died.

"You could have been killed in that terrible city," your father says.

"Boston's a fine city if it weren't for the British troops," you say. "We should have the right to make our own laws here in the colonies."

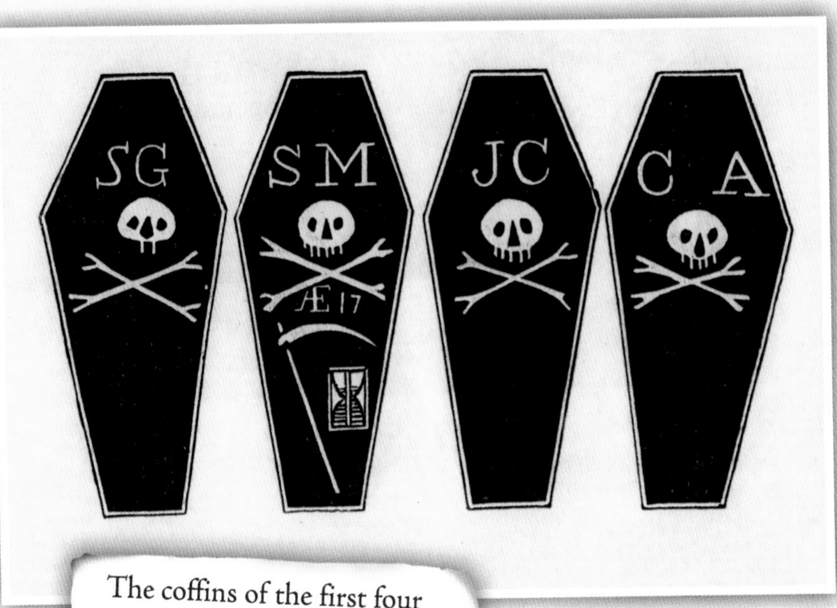

The coffins of the first four massacre victims were labeled with their initials.

"Someday, we may have that right," Father replies. "But until then, you made the right decision to leave Boston."

THE END

To follow another path, turn to page 13.
To read the conclusion, turn to page 103.

You run for the doctor. "You're needed at Mr. Payne's," you say. He dashes off in that direction.

When you return home, everyone gathers around as you tell your tale. Even Mr. Hancock listens intently. "I've met with the other leaders of the Sons of Liberty," he tells you. "Tomorrow, we're demanding that the soldiers leave Boston."

THE END

To follow another path, turn to page 13.
To read the conclusion, turn to page 103.

Cook locks the door as the bells stop ringing. "Maybe the worst is over," she says. A short while later, there's a knock on the door. It's Sarah, in tears. There's blood on her cape. "Are you hurt?" you ask.

"It's Sam," she cries. "He's been killed by the British soldiers." Cook fixes Sarah a cup of Labrador tea, and you try to comfort her.

Between sobs, Sarah tells you the story. "Sam and the others threatened the soldiers, but only with words. Sam wasn't even armed. Some of the apprentices threw rocks and snowballs, and someone yelled, 'Fire!' Now Sam's gone forever. I hope to see those soldiers hang."

THE END

To follow another path, turn to page 13.
To read the conclusion, turn to page 103.

You run out to join the crowd. You're pushed along toward the Custom House on King Street.

You stand at the back of the crowd. About 100 people are shouting and throwing rocks and ice at a small group of soldiers. One man yells, "Fire! I dare you." A moment later, a gun goes off. Then you hear several more shots.

The crowd moves back. The bodies of the dead and wounded lie in the snowy street. You race for home. Thomas is waiting for you in the kitchen. You rush into his arms, sobbing.

Later, you learn five men were killed. "What if it had been you?" you ask Thomas.

"They died for the cause of liberty," he says. "Many more may die before the battle is won."

THE END

To follow another path, turn to page 13.
To read the conclusion, turn to page 103.

You wait at Mr. Hancock's house for Thomas. Is he lost? When you hear gunshots in the distance, you panic. What if he's been shot?

You dash into the street, but there is no sign of Thomas. You run toward the noise. Thomas staggers toward you. He has blood on his shirt. "Trouble on King Street," he gasps. "I was on my way here when soldiers started shooting into a crowd. A man standing beside me fell. I'm not sure if he was dead or just wounded. Others were shot as well."

"But you're not hurt?" you ask.

"No. I'm fine. But we can't stay here. Boston is a dangerous place. Tomorrow, we'll go back to Lexington, where all will be peaceful."

THE END

To follow another path, turn to page 13.
To read the conclusion, turn to page 103.

Samuel Adams (left) met with British governor Thomas Hutchinson (right) after the massacre.

CHAPTER 5

Aftermath of the Massacre

At the time of the Boston Massacre, Massachusetts law included the Riot Act. This law allowed police to break up a gathering of 12 or more armed people or 50 or more unarmed people. To do this, police read the Riot Act to the crowd.

On the night of March 5, 1770, no one read the Riot Act. Townspeople were then within their rights to gather in the streets.

But the townspeople weren't blameless, either. The soldiers held their tempers and their guns despite the crowd's taunting. But at some point, the soldiers thought they heard Preston give an order to shoot. That's when they opened fire. Crispus Attucks, Samuel Gray, and James Caldwell were killed at the scene. Patrick Carr and Samuel Maverick were wounded and died later. Edward Payne, Christopher Monk, John Clark, John Green, Robert Patterson, and David Parker were wounded but recovered.

After the Massacre, Boston's leaders demanded that the troops leave Boston. On March 6, acting governor Thomas Hutchinson asked the army commanding officer to move the troops to Castle William. This fort was on an island in Boston Harbor. During the next week, the troops were moved to the crowded fort.

After the shootings, the Sons of Liberty gathered eyewitness reports. Paul Revere distributed his famous engraving of the events. Revere wasn't there, but he based his engraving on a drawing by Henry Pelham. Word of the shootings spread throughout the colonies.

Captain Preston and the soldiers remained in prison awaiting trial. Boston lawyers John Adams and Josiah Quincy agreed to represent the men. Boston's leaders were eager to prove that Boston supported justice and fairness for all.

Preston's trial lasted from October 24 to October 30, 1770. John Adams pointed out that the witnesses did not agree on what happened. The jurors found Preston not guilty.

In late November, the other soldiers went on trial. The jury found six of the soldiers not guilty. These soldiers immediately returned to Great Britain. The jury found Hugh Montgomery and Matthew Killroy guilty of manslaughter. They were branded on their thumbs and sent back to Britain.

No one knows exactly what happened on the night of March 5, 1770. There was much confusion, and witnesses told different stories. But the event remains an important part of American history. Samuel Adams said that the Boston Massacre laid the foundation for American independence.

On April 19, 1775, the first battles of the Revolutionary War were fought in Lexington and Concord, Massachusetts. On July 4, 1776, members of the Second Continental Congress adopted the Declaration of Independence.

Many bloody battles followed until the British surrendered in October 1781. On September 3, 1783, the war officially ended with the signing of the Treaty of Paris. At last, the United States of America was a free and independent country.

On April 19, 1775, American soldiers won the first battles of the Revolutionary War.

Timeline

October 1, 1768 — British troops arrive in Boston.

February 22, 1770 — Ebenezer Richardson shoots and kills Christopher Seider.

February 26, 1770 — About 2,000 people attend Seider's funeral.

March 2 and 3, 1770 — Soldiers and ropeworkers fight at Gray's Ropeworks.

March 5, 1770 — British soldiers clash with patriots in several areas of Boston. At the Custom House, Boston residents Crispus Attucks, Samuel Gray, and James Caldwell are shot and killed. Samuel Maverick, Patrick Carr, Edward Payne, and five other men are wounded.

March 6, 1770 — Maverick dies; Captain Thomas Preston is arrested; eight other soldiers turn themselves in; patriot leaders demand that troops leave Boston.

March 10–14, 1770 — British troops are sent to Castle William in Boston Harbor.

March 14, 1770 — Patrick Carr dies, bringing the number of victims to five.

April 1770 — Ebenezer Richardson is found guilty of murdering Christopher Seider, but is later pardoned.

October 30, 1770 — Captain Preston is found not guilty.

December 5, 1770 — Six soldiers are found not guilty. Two are convicted of manslaughter.

December 16, 1773 — Patriots protest the tea tax during the Boston Tea Party.

April 19, 1775 — The Battles of Lexington and Concord are the first battles of the Revolutionary War.

July 4, 1776 — Members of the Second Continental Congress adopt the Declaration of Independence.

September 3, 1783 — The Revolutionary War officially ends; the United States of America is an independent country.

Other Paths to Explore

In this book you've seen how the events surrounding the Boston Massacre look different from three points of view.

Perspectives on history are as varied as the people who lived it. You can explore other paths on your own to learn more about what happened. Seeing history from many points of view is an important part of understanding it.

Here are some ideas for other Boston Massacre points of view to explore:

- At the time of the Boston Massacre, slavery was legal in the colonies. What would it be like to be a slave in a country that is fighting for its freedom?

- Not everyone in the colonies supported the Sons of Liberty. What would it be like to be loyal to Great Britain during that time?

- People living in Great Britain likely didn't understand why the colonists were angry. If you were living in Britain at that time, how would you have reacted?

The Battle of Bunker Hill:

An Interactive History Adventure

By Michael Burgan

Consultant:
Len Travers
Associate Professor of History
University of Massachusetts at Dartmouth

Table of Contents

About Your Adventure

YOU are in Boston as the Revolutionary War begins. The British are attacking a patriot fort just outside the city. The city is divided between British Loyalists and American rebels. Which side are you on? And can you survive?

In this book you'll explore how the choices people made meant the difference between life and death. The events you'll experience happened to real people.

Chapter One sets the scene. Then you choose which path to read. Follow the directions at the bottom of each page. The choices you make will change your outcome. After you finish one path, go back and read the others for new perspectives and more adventures.

YOU CHOOSE the path

you take through history.

American militia and British soldiers first battled near the towns of Lexington and Concord.

CHAPTER 1

The Path to War

All of Boston buzzes with news from yesterday, April 19, 1775. British troops and American militia battled outside the city. You try to do what you normally do. But not much has been normal in Boston for a long time.

For almost seven years, British soldiers have been living in and around the city. The Americans call them "Redcoats" and "Lobsterbacks" because of the long red jackets they wear. The soldiers make sure the colonists follow the laws passed by the British parliament.

Turn the page.

The harbor made Boston a busy colonial port city.

It was different during the French and Indian War (1754–1763). Then King George's soldiers defended the colonies. Now, many colonists are tired of British control. For one thing, taxes keep going up and the colonists have no say. Some colonists want to break ties with the king. They call themselves patriots.

Other colonists like being British. These Loyalists think King George has a strong army and good trade ties. Loyalists wish the rebel patriots could work with the king.

In 1773, some patriots threw crates of tea into the harbor in protest of a tea tax. The British parliament responded with more laws. The relationship between the colonists and Britain has not improved.

On April 18, 1775, General Thomas Gage sent British troops to Concord. They tried to take patriot weapons and destroy battle supplies.

Patriots Paul Revere and William Dawes spread the word that British troops were coming. Patriots turned out to fight the British near Lexington and near Concord. No one knows who fired the first shot. But the battle raged all day.

Turn the page.

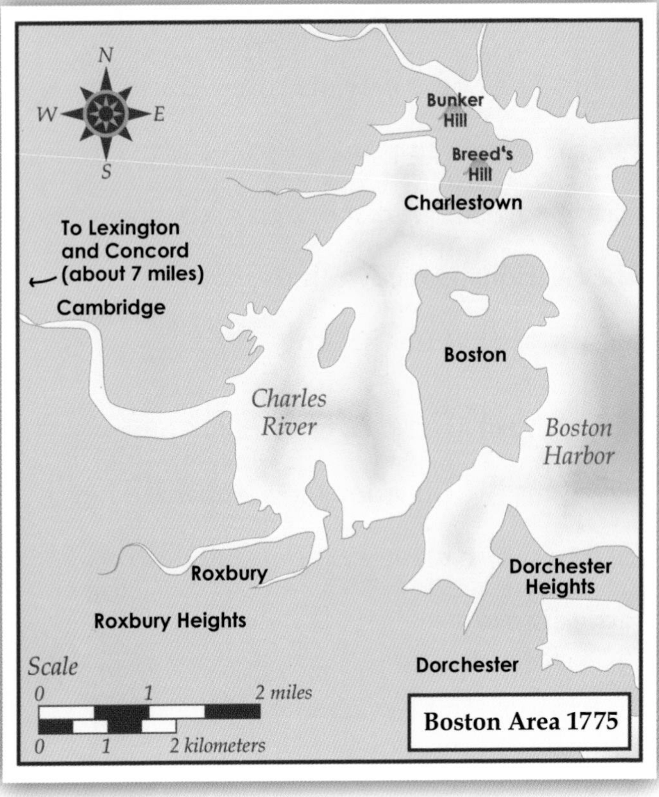

Wounded British soldiers are still making their way to Boston. You hear the British soldiers talk. They are amazed the patriots fought so well. They are eager for revenge.

You also learn that thousands of patriot soldiers are coming. They're from across Massachusetts and parts of New England.

General Artemus Ward and his men are in Cambridge, just west of Charlestown. Patriot troops are also heading south to Roxbury. The patriots plan to start a siege of Boston. Goods and supplies will not be able to get into Boston. The British troops will be surrounded.

Of course, colonists living in Boston get most of their goods from British ships too. No one knows how life is going to change now that war has come to Boston. One thing is clear—another battle is coming soon. What will you do?

To fight in the Battle of Bunker Hill as a patriot soldier, turn to page **123**.

To fight in the Battle of Bunker Hill as a British soldier, turn to page **155**.

To see the Battle of Bunker Hill through a Boston civilian's eyes, turn to page **183**.

Many patriot soldiers left their farms to join the militia.

CHAPTER 2

Patriots: Pursuing Liberty

You're not a professional soldier. Like most patriots, you're a simple farmer. But you want freedom from the British. After the Battles of Lexington and Concord, you decided to join the militia. You left Boston and went to train in Cambridge. For two months now, you have been training here.

It's evening now in Cambridge. Being away from your family and your farm is hard. You stay in a home that once belonged to a Loyalist. Many Loyalists fled Cambridge soon after the Lexington and Concord battles.

Turn the page.

You take some leftover bread from your pocket. Each day, patriot soldiers are given a pound of meat and a pound of bread. You sit down to eat a few slices and start writing a letter to your wife. You ask her to send a fresh shirt. All the marching drills and shooting practice dirties your clothes quickly. The day doesn't allow much time for washing. A clean, mended shirt would sure feel good.

You have heard that the British armies have women traveling with them. They mend and wash for the soldiers. That would be nice, but you wouldn't want your wife to be so close to danger.

On the morning street patrol, you overhear townspeople talking.

"Did you know General Gage is planning to move some Redcoats out of Boston?"

"Yes," the other replies, "I heard he plans to take them to Dorchester."

You know Dorchester is on high ground just south of Boston. The patriots would like control of that area. It would help in the siege of Boston. With a few cannons, patriots could trap British boats in the harbor. The British must not be allowed to take that hill.

Turn the page.

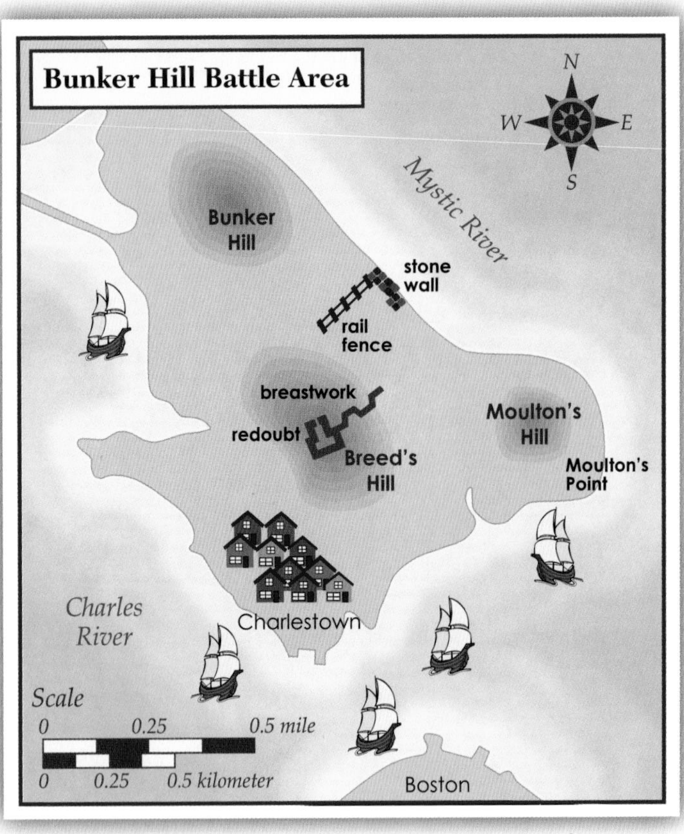

By the time you return from patrol, General Ward has orders for the patriots to strike from the north first. Ward directs Colonel William Prescott to lead about 1,000 men to Bunker Hill. The men will build a small fort called a redoubt.

It's only a couple of miles march from Cambridge to the hill. But you will need to work fast. The British already have ships in the area. And it will not take long for the Redcoats in Boston to row across the half mile of water. Will you join Prescott in his mission?

To go with the soldiers headed to Bunker Hill, turn to page **128.**

To remain with the troops staying in Cambridge, turn to page **140.**

You carry your shovel and your musket. It's late on the night of June 16, 1775, and Colonel Prescott leads you and the others out of Cambridge. You meet up with 200 troops from Connecticut led by General Israel Putnam. Putnam, Prescott, and Richard Gridley, a military engineer, decide to send troops to Breed's Hill instead of Bunker Hill. It is closer to Boston.

Gridley outlines where the redoubt will go on the hill. You take your shovel and begin digging. The dirt forms the walls of the redoubt. Other men build a barrier called a breastwork. It extends beyond one of the walls. As you work, Colonel Prescott walks up and down the trenches. He tells you, "Faster—we must finish before sunrise. And be as quiet as possible! We don't want the British to know what we're doing."

Prescott and his men sneaked up Breed's Hill in the dark.

You haven't slept all night, and you haven't eaten since this afternoon. Your throat is dry, and you ache for water. But you ignore all that and obey Prescott's order. You dig as quietly as you can. You put your shovel into the earth over and over.

Turn the page.

Around 4:00 in the morning, a loud noise makes you look up. "Cannon fire!" a soldier cries, "From a ship in the harbor!"

The cannons fire again. Your friend Asa Pollard is working outside the redoubt wall. An iron cannon ball hits him. He' s been killed. You and the other soldiers stand quiet. You're reminded that war has deadly consequences.

Colonel Prescott jumps up on the redoubt's dirt wall. "Come on, men," he yells. He ignores the cannon balls still flying through the air. "Keep working."

Some men have already left Breed's Hill. They have sneaked away when no one was looking. They fear a British attack on the redoubt. You're afraid too. But you know Colonel Prescott wants you to keep digging.

If you follow Prescott's order and keep digging, turn to page **132**.

If you ignore his order, turn to page **134**.

You keep digging as the sun rises in the sky. Throughout the morning, more patriot troops arrive. Some join the Connecticut troops, who have built a second breastwork of stone and wood. Troops from New Hampshire have also built a stone wall nearby. One of the new arrivals is Dr. Joseph Warren. He is a respected leader in Boston and a devoted patriot. You tell a friend, "If Dr. Warren is ready to risk his life here, then so am I."

All this time, British cannons fire. As the day goes on, you see small boats carrying Redcoats to the shore. Some climb out of the boats and begin marching toward Breed's Hill. Other troops head for the rail fence and the stone wall. The British will attack soon.

Dr. Joseph Warren (right) joined Prescott and the patriots at the redoubt.

To defend the redoubt against the British troops, turn to page **142**.

To face the British at the rail fence and stone wall, turn to page **149**.

You've changed your mind about fighting. Your family needs you back on the farm. You don't want to risk dying in battle.

When no one is looking, you drop your shovel and slowly move away from the redoubt. Looking around, you see other soldiers doing the same thing. You make your way back to Bunker Hill. A little later, you see men leaving Breed's Hill carrying shovels and picks.

"What's going on?" you ask.

"General Putnam wants us to build another breastwork here."

Some of the men begin to dig at Bunker Hill. Others, though, head past the hill and continue back toward Cambridge. You keep walking.

As you walk, you see more troops coming from Cambridge. They are heading toward the redoubt. They're ready to fight—and perhaps die—for the patriot cause. One calls out to you, "Where are you going? The British are going to land."

"I'm too tired," you reply. "I've been digging all night and I haven't had water for hours."

"That's no excuse," another soldier says. "Come with us."

If you continue to go to Cambridge, turn to page **136**.

If you join the troops going to Breed's Hill, turn to page **139**.

The soldiers continue to stream past you, heading to Breed's Hill. The one who stopped you waits for an answer. "I'm sorry, but I can't go with you," you finally say. You look around. Other soldiers stream off the hill, looking for safety. Like you, they don't want to end up dead—like Asa Pollard. The British cannons still boom. Many men want to get as far from them as possible.

You continue walking to Cambridge. Some patriot soldiers come toward you, pulling four cannons. They are much smaller than the British guns pounding away at Breed's Hill. "We'll never stop the British with those puny cannons," you think to yourself.

Finally, with the hot June sun beating down, you reach town. You see more men preparing to march off to battle.

Others are trying to find wagons to bring supplies. Your stomach grumbles, reminding you that you haven't eaten yet today. You head for your camp, knowing your next meal is close by. But the men on Breed's Hill will have a long wait before they eat again.

You feel guilty that you left the battlefield. But you're eager to see your family again. You hope that the war will end soon, so you can go back to your regular life.

THE END

To follow another path, turn to page 121.
To read the conclusion, turn to page 213.

Patriot soldiers waited for the British to march up the hill.

You turn around and join the men marching toward Breed's Hill. You believe in the patriot cause of freedom. You are tired and thirsty, but you want to do your part. You are glad to see that a lot of work has gone on since the early morning.

A stone wall and a rail fence form a breastwork that runs from the Mystic River toward the redoubt. Men from New Hampshire and Connecticut stand ready at these posts. Regiments from Massachusetts head to the redoubt and the breastwork right near it.

Turn to page **142**.

You watch the men go off to Bunker Hill. Then you go to bed. On the morning of June 17, the distant sound of booming cannons wakes you up early. British ships in the harbor are firing on Charlestown. You check your musket and wait with the other soldiers. You know General Ward is at his headquarters, waiting for news from Colonel Prescott.

The soldiers wonder what will happen.

"The Redcoats will attack Cambridge," one says. "Ward has got to keep us here."

"But those men on Bunker Hill can't go it alone," you reply. "He has to send more troops."

Soon General Ward decides to send some New Hampshire men to help Prescott. Prescott and his men have actually built the redoubt on Breed's Hill instead of Bunker Hill. The New Hampshire troops have built a stone wall near the Mystic River, north of the redoubt. Connecticut and Massachusetts regiments head to the redoubt. In either place, the fighting could be fierce.

To join the Massachusetts regiments at the redoubt on Breed's Hill, turn to page **142**.

To join the New Hampshire regiments at the stone wall, turn to page **149**.

The redoubt is small, but the walls are thick. This fort will provide good defense against the British soldiers who have started their march from the beach.

It's now about 3:30 in the afternoon, and the June sun is beating down on you. The temperature has soared to 95 degrees. Your broad-brimmed hat helps keep the sun's heat off your face. You see a wave of British soldiers head toward a rail fence where the Connecticut troops are hiding in the grass. The Redcoats also don't seem to see the New Hampshire regiment. They are behind a stone wall they built this morning from tide rocks. The patriots open fire quickly, killing several dozen British troops.

At the same time, a group of Redcoats has made it up through the tall grass and over the rocky ground. They are nearing your position in the redoubt. You quickly pack your musket with gunpowder and a lead ball.

"Fire!" Colonel Prescott shouts.

You pull the trigger, and your musket jerks upward in your hands. Other guns around you go off at the same time. Clouds of smoke form from the exploding gunpowder. Many of the British have been hit. You reload your musket and fire again. Dozens of dead British soldiers now lie around the redoubt.

Turn the page.

You join the other men in a cheer, as the British stopped their advance. But a larger force soon heads toward the redoubt. You go to reload again, but a sharp, hot pain fills your arm.

"I've been hit," you cry.

A soldier at your side helps wrap a cloth around your wound. As you sit down, you see that the British have retreated again. But no one thinks they have given up.

Around you, the patriots reload their muskets. Someone tells you to leave the redoubt and retreat back to Bunker Hill. You want to stay and fight, but the pain is getting worse.

Soldiers used their guns as clubs and swords when they got close to the enemy.

If you stay to continue fighting, turn to page **146**.

If you decide to retreat, turn to page **153**.

Staying to fight is the honorable thing to do, you decide. Your arm hurts too much for you to hold your gun, but you help bring gunpowder to some men who have run out. The supplies are now almost gone. You search the ground for nails or other bits of metal that the others can fire from their guns.

Only about an hour has passed since the fighting started. But to you it feels like days. Around 4:30 in the afternoon, you see the British advance a third time. They march in a single rank. The patriots fire the nails. Others throw rocks. But nothing stops the British this time. They charge over the redoubt walls. They stab the men around you with their bayonets. Men you have trained with for weeks are now dead at your feet.

Dr. Joseph Warren was shot while defending the redoubt.

Some of the patriots begin to run toward Bunker Hill. Others keep fighting even as the British pour over the wall. Colonel Prescott uses his sword to push away enemy bayonets. You quickly try to crawl away. You turn and see Dr. Warren leaving the redoubt. A British soldier shoots the brave leader. He falls to the ground.

Turn the page.

In the same moment, a British soldier lunges at you with his bayonet. You've been stabbed in the heart. As you take your last breath, you know have given your life for the great cause of American freedom.

THE END

To follow another path, turn to page 121.
To read the conclusion, turn to page 213.

The morning low tide exposed a lot of stone and rock. Patriots quickly piled it together to form another defense. The stone wall extends to a nearby rail fence overgrown with grass. The stone wall and fence should keep the British from just going around the redoubt.

You take your place behind the stone wall. Soon, Colonel John Stark gives orders to prepare for a British attack. You pack gunpowder and a lead ball into your musket. Colonel Stark jumps over the wall. He walks about 40 yards out and drives a stake in the ground. When he returns he says, "Not a man is to fire until the first Redcoat crosses the stake." Stark wants to make sure you will not waste ammunition. You must hit your targets.

Turn the page.

Hundreds of British troops have now landed on the beach. They leave their boats and approach the wall. Fifteen Redcoats march side by side, 20 rows deep. As they pass the stake in the ground, Stark motions for you to fire. You pull the trigger and feel the kick from your musket. All around you, other guns go off at the same time.

The patriots shot down the British soldiers one row at a time.

You look through the cloud of smoke from the guns. British soldiers lie dead or dying. Still, others keep marching toward the wall.

Another group of patriot soldiers fires their guns, and then a third. With each round of firing, more Redcoats fall to the ground. The troops behind them can't move past the bodies, and they begin to retreat.

The patriots at the redoubt are also driving off the British. You hear their cheer of success and you feel good too. Colonel Stark walks along the wall. He says, "The fighting's not done yet, lads. The Redcoats will be back."

Soon you see Stark is right. The British attack the rail fence near the stone wall. You fire at them, as do the defenders at the fence. Once again, the British quickly retreat.

Turn the page.

Sweat rolls down your face. You have been in the sun for hours. Around 4:30 in the afternoon, another group of Redcoats starts coming toward the stone wall. A much larger force is also attacking the redoubt.

As you reload your musket, a shot hits you in the arm. As you slump down, you see the British storm the redoubt. The patriots there begin to retreat to Bunker Hill. Colonel Stark orders all of you to retreat as well.

Holding your wounded arm, you retreat to Bunker Hill. Patriots there have dug trenches as another line of defense. You watch the patriot defenses crumble at the Breed's Hill redoubt. The British soon attack Bunker Hill. "Stand and give them one more shot," General Putnam cries.

It is no use. The British soon overrun Bunker Hill too. The patriots retreat further. But the British troops do not follow. They have taken the redoubt. And they have lost too many men to keep fighting.

That night, a doctor treats your wound. You can only think that the patriots have lost badly at the Battle of Bunker Hill. But you and the patriots will not quit the fight for freedom.

THE END

To follow another path, turn to page 121.
To read the conclusion, turn to page 213.

European battle style had soldiers march in rows.

CHAPTER 3

British Soldiers: Keeping the Colonies

At sunrise on the morning of June 17, you wake to the sound of cannon fire. Even from your quarters in Boston, the noise is enough to get your attention.

"It's our ships," someone says. "They're firing on the colonist rebels." Overnight, the rebels began building a small fort called a redoubt. The fort is on a hill near Charlestown.

For weeks you've waited for another chance to fight the rebel Americans. You still see the image of your friends dying on the way back from Concord. Since then, several thousand British soldiers have arrived from England.

Turn the page.

"Prepare for battle!" The order comes down from your regiment leader. You put on your red coat and tall, pointed black hat. You tie up your long hair with a ribbon. Next you strap on belts that hold your bayonet and the cartridges for your gun. Then you sling over your back the pack that holds extra clothes, food, water, and other supplies.

It takes nearly three hours to organize all the soldiers for fighting. You're ready to get to the battle.

General William Howe will lead the first attack on Charlestown. General Henry Clinton will remain behind and command reinforcements.

To follow the soldiers who go with Howe, go on to page **157**.

To follow the reinforcements under Clinton, turn to page **170**.

It's about noon as your regiment boards a rowboat. You count another 27 boats in the water from Boston to Charlestown, less than a half mile away. The boats head for a spot called Moulton's Point. British ships keep firing cannons to keep the beach clear of rebels.

By 3:00 in the afternoon, all the men have crossed the water. General Howe divides his forces. He takes your regiment and several others to attack a stone wall and rail fence north of the redoubt. General Robert Pigot heads left toward the fort itself. As Pigot's men march away, shots ring out from some buildings in Charlestown. Rebel shooters are hiding there. Howe orders the town destroyed and set on fire. As you march into battle, you see smoke begin to rise from the town.

Turn the page.

Drums play as you march side by side with the other soldiers. Ahead and behind you are more rows of British troops. You move slowly. The ground is covered with rocks and holes that you can't easily see in the tall grass. The pack on your back weighs at least 60 pounds. It feels extra heavy because of the hot June sun. Still, the guns from the British ships keep booming. You keep marching toward the wall.

Suddenly, as you near the wall, the rebels begin to fire. You see men ahead of you fall to the ground. Some are dead. Some are wounded. A sergeant near you shouts, "Come on, soldiers, keep marching!"

You watch as men around you are shot and killed. You could be killed too if you keep moving. But if you don't follow orders, you could be whipped as punishment. What do you do?

If you turn back, turn to page **160**.

If you keep marching, turn to page **164**.

Long grass, bumpy ground, and dead bodies made it hard for the Redcoats to keep marching.

The sight of all the dead soldiers is too much to bear. You break out of the line and run across the field. Your foot catches in a hole. You fall and hit your head on a stone. You feel blood on your head, but you get up and run.

On the shore, you see other infantrymen who have fled the battle. Some have wounds. Most are scared.

They never thought the rebels could shoot so well. Some of the men crowd into the boats hoping to hide. Officers come by, yelling "Get out, you cowards! This battle isn't over yet."

One officer pushes you with his sword. "You too, soldier. You're going again. General Howe wants to make another go at the fence."

You point at the wound on your head. "I've been shot," you lie. "I need to go back to Boston."

The officer looks at you closely. "There are men still out there with worse injuries. Are you that much of a coward?"

If you still don't want to fight, turn to page **162**.

If you decide to fight, turn to page **163**.

"I . . . I'm not a coward," you say. "But this wound . . ."

"All right, all right," the officer says with disgust. "Get on the boat."

Within a few minutes, the boat is filled with wounded men. Some moan in pain. Others are barely alive. As you sail toward Boston, you hear the sound of guns and see the sky fill with smoke. Perhaps you were a coward. But at least you are alive.

THE END

To follow another path, turn to page 121.
To read the conclusion, turn to page 213.

You start to feel bad about running away from the battle. Men you know have died bravely, while you're afraid to do your duty. You decide that you must act with honor. If you don't keep your service to the king, you are no better than the rebel colonists.

"Maybe the wound is not so bad after all," you say.

"I thought so," the officer said. "Go on, get out there."

You head back to the beach where most of the men are waiting for orders. You prepare for another attack on the fence.

Turn to page **168**.

British soldiers assembled on the beach between their attacks on Breed's Hill.

The rebel guns continue to fire as you move forward. At times, you step across dead British soldiers who were your friends. You hear an order to stop and fire. Your shot has no effect. The rebel soldiers are safely behind the wall and fence.

As you reach for another cartridge for your gun, an officer calls out, "Pull back! Back to the beach!"

You turn to run and cross back over the rocky ground. A voice screams, "Help me!"

You look down and see a soldier from your regiment. He is lying on the ground. Blood flows from his chest.

"Help me," he begs. "I'll never make it back to the boats alone."

The rebel guns are still firing. If you stop to help, you could be killed. But you know you would want someone to help you if you were wounded.

To help the soldier, turn to page **166**.

To keep retreating, turn to page **168**.

The wounded soldier stares up at you. He is pleading.

"All right, hold on," you say.

You kneel by the soldier to help him up. His clothes are soaked with blood. You struggle to your feet, holding him with your right arm. Slowly you begin to half-drag and half-carry him across the field. After only a few steps, you feel a hot, piercing pain in your left leg.

"I'm shot!" you cry.

You struggle to keep your balance. The pain makes your head pound. The wounded soldier is getting weaker. He starts to drag his feet.

"Come on," you say. "We can make it."

After a few minutes, you see the boats on the shore. The soldier is still breathing, but just barely. Blood is still flowing from your wound, but you think you can reach the boat. Now you hope you live until you reach the hospital back in Boston.

THE END

To follow another path, turn to page 121.
To read the conclusion, turn to page 213.

On the beach, you see General Howe. He is stunned at the losses and the rebel defense. Within 15 minutes, Howe has prepared those left for another attack on the fence. Your regiment begins marching again.

Once again, you march in line. Fifes and drums play as you walk over and around the men who have already died. The order comes, "Prepare for a bayonet charge."

As you wait for the order to charge, a rebel officer yells, "Fire!" Gunshots break out. Soldiers once again fall around you. You move to the side, but the rebels continue to fire. General Howe stands in the middle of the smoke and bloodshed.

"Once more, men," he cries, "once more. Show them what British soldiers can do."

General Howe was surprised at how well the patriots defended Breed's Hill.

The enemy fire is too heavy for you to reach the fence and use your bayonet. You decide to stop and shoot instead. You take aim at one of the defenders behind a rail. The shot hits its target. Before you can reload, a musket ball strikes you. You are killed instantly.

THE END

To follow another path, turn to page 121.
To read the conclusion, turn to page 213.

You wait in Boston for your orders to sail. Boats full of wounded soldiers keep returning across the harbor. These men were hit during in first attack on the redoubt. You help carry the men. You hear hundreds of guns fire during a second attack. Then there is silence, except for the booming of cannons and the cries of more men in pain.

Around 4:00 in the afternoon, General Clinton orders your regiment to sail to Moulton's Point. General Clinton climbs into the lead boat. As the boats approach the shore, musket balls are fired at you.

Several men in General Clinton's boat are shot. General Clinton ignores the gunfire. He jumps onto the shore. He sends some of the men to support General Howe at Breed's Hill. General Clinton takes command of everyone else on the beach.

To fight under Clinton's command,
turn to page **172**.

To go help fight under Howe's command,
turn to page **174**.

General Clinton begins organizing the men on the beach. He also calls out to the men wounded in the earlier battles.

"I know you've advanced two times already. And we've suffered great losses. But we must take that redoubt! If you can walk and hold a gun, follow me."

You help one or two of the wounded struggle to their feet. General Clinton forms all the soldiers into lines on the beach. You will help General Robert Pigot, who has been attacking the redoubt.

Pigot's men have already suffered heavy casualties during the two attacks. At 4:30 in the afternoon, the third attack on the redoubt begins. Your rank marches past dead British soldiers. You know your own life could end at any moment. But you will fight to the end. The order comes to prepare for a bayonet charge. Other soldiers fall in front of you, hit by rebel gunfire. But you keep running and reach the wall of the redoubt.

Turn to page **176**.

Despite the heavy losses, British soldiers continued to attack.

For the first two attacks, the men carried their heavy packs. This time, you are told to leave your packs behind. Without the extra weight, you'll be able to move more easily. Some of the men take off their red coats as well. It helps to ease the blistering heat.

You look out over the field you must cross to reach the redoubt. Dead British soldiers lie in heaps. The drums begin to play. You march out toward the rebels. Rebel shots take down some of the men in front. Others step up to take their place.

The British artillery keeps firing at the small fort. Smoke from exploding gunpowder floats over the field. "Push on, push on!" some soldiers holler around you. You attach your bayonet blade to the end of your gun.

Turn the page.

British soldiers attached long blades called bayonets to their guns.

You climb over the wall of the redoubt with your bayonet in front of you. The rebels are running out of ammunition. An American swings at your head with his musket. You use your bayonet to fight off the patriot.

British soldiers are storming into the redoubt from three sides. Many of the rebels flee. Others lay dead on the ground. You turn to attack a rebel before he can escape. At that moment, you feel a powerful thud. The clubbing blow drops you to your knees in pain. You struggle to your feet. Touching the side of your head, you feel blood. Angry, you want to keep fighting. But you know you could be killed if you can't defend yourself.

If you keep fighting, turn to page **178.**

If you seek help for your wound, turn to page **180.**

You don't have to worry about another rebel hitting you. As you look around, you see only British troops left in the redoubt. The rebels are running back to Bunker Hill. You join troops chasing the enemy.

A few rebel shots fire as you near Bunker Hill. You charge with your bayonet. The rebels retreat from the hill. Soon, the British soldiers have control of Bunker Hill as well.

You help some men bring cannons to the top of the hill. The guns fire at the retreating rebels. British ships also aim at the rebels as they flee. The battle is over, but your day is not. You have orders to begin building a new fort on Bunker Hill. The war against the rebels is just beginning.

THE END

To follow another path, turn to page 121.
To read the conclusion, turn to page 213.

Wounded British soldiers were brought to Boston all through the night.

You climb out of the redoubt and walk back toward the beach. Another soldier helps you bandage your head. You see that you're lucky. Many of the men have worse wounds than you. You board a boat to cross the harbor. The bottom is covered in blood from the other wounded men it has already carried today.

You reach the docks in Boston. Wagons are waiting. Civilians have come out to help bring the wounded to hospitals. Even wheelbarrows are used to carry the injured men.

You're able to walk to the hospital. Along the way, you see your sergeant. His arm is in a sling.

"Are you all right, soldier?" he asks.

"Yes, Sergeant. And you?"

He holds up the injured arm. "Not too bad. Just missing a bit of flesh."

"How did we do, sir?" you ask.

"We won the battle today, but this war is far from over."

You keep walking, wondering if you will be lucky enough to survive another battle like this one.

THE END

To follow another path, turn to page 121.
To read the conclusion, turn to page 213.

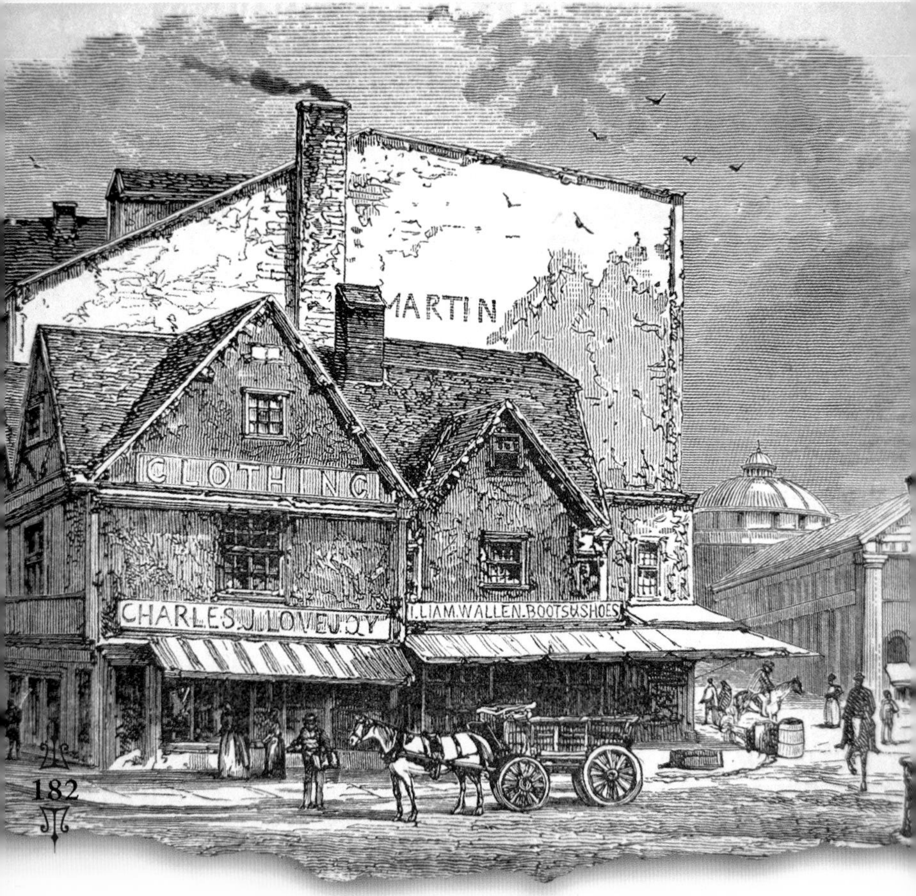

British soldiers occupied Boston and tried to enforce laws passed by the British parliament.

Life in Boston

You see many changes in Boston in the weeks after the battle of April 19, 1775. Some of your friends have left the city. They fear the patriots will attack the Redcoats in Boston. At the same time, several thousand Loyalists stream into the capital. Patriots forced them from their homes because they support the British. The Loyalists believe they'll be safe in Boston. The British guns can protect them.

You're still not sure what you and your family should do. Your best friend decides to help the patriots.

Turn the page.

"Come with me," your friend says. "Bring your family and all that you can carry in your wagon. Get out of Boston."

"I don't know," you say. "You really think the patriots are fighting for a good cause?"

"Of course," he says. "They're fighting to protect our liberty. We can't elect our own leaders, like we always did before. And don't forget the laws they passed after the tea went in the harbor—the Intolerable Acts."

"That's true," you reply. "I've been worrying about being told to house British soldiers."

"Only the patriots," says your friend, "will make sure we have our rights again. The king and his men—they don't care about us over here in America."

"The British government is the best in the world," you say. "We still have plenty of freedom."

You friend shakes his head. "If the patriots lose, the British will keep taking away more rights. I'm going to Cambridge to fight for our liberty."

To support the patriots, turn to page **186**.

To be a Loyalist in support of the British, turn to page **198**.

You decide that your friend is right. But you're not ready to leave Boston. You fear Loyalists or thieves will take what you leave behind. You send your family to Cambridge. They'll be safer there. Any fighting will likely be closer to the harbor. And with the patriot siege, goods are only going to get harder to find.

In June you go out to a local tavern with some friends. "I heard some Redcoats talking," says one friend. "They think they'll be sent to Dorchester soon."

"The patriots need to control Dorchester," you say. "With a few large cannons, they could trap British boats in the harbor." If the British take Dorchester, the patriot siege of Boston would be unsuccessful.

You know that the patriots need this information. But you have no safe way to get out of Boston. General Gage will not approve travel passes for patriots to leave the city. If you try to sneak out, you could be arrested.

To leave Boston and give the patriots the information, turn to page **188**.

To stay in Boston, turn to page **196**.

You decide the information is worth the risk. You dress as a fisherman and borrow a friend's rowboat. At nightfall, you cross the water. Luckily, no soldiers are along the shore. You head for Charlestown, since the town is almost empty. Most people have left in case more fighting breaks out. You walk the 3 miles from Charlestown to Cambridge. When you reach town, you see a patriot officer and give him your information.

The next day, you travel through Roxbury and across the Boston Neck. As you enter the city, some Loyalists recognize you. They know you are a patriot and should not have been allowed out of Boston. One of the men starts talking to a soldier on Cornhill Street. You turn around and begin to walk quickly in the other direction.

"Halt!" the soldier commands. You stop. With his large black hat, the soldier seems to tower over you.

"Were you just outside Boston?" the soldier asks. "Tell me what you were doing."

You look up at the officer and lie. "My family is in Cambridge. My son was sick. I needed to see him."

"All right," the officer says. "Be on your way."

As you walk away, you see the Loyalists glaring at you. You know they will be watching you closely. You decide you must leave Boston. That night, you leave for Cambridge again. But this time, you won't come back to Boston.

Turn the page.

Colonial women feared losing their husbands in battle.

You find your family. They are staying with a group of friends from Boston. "You should join our regiment and fight with us," one man says.

"Who would take care of my wife and children?" you say. "I'd have to leave my family."

"Yes, we all have families. Fighting this war is the only way to protect our freedom and the freedom of our families," another adds.

You look over at your wife. She is almost crying. She fears being alone if you're killed in battle. Yet you know how important it is to defeat the British.

If you decide to fight, turn to page **192**.

If you decide not to fight, turn to page **194**.

You hug your wife before heading off. You tell her, "I must do my part, dear. I must fight."

You are welcomed into the regiment, but they don't have a musket for you. The patriots are low on many supplies, including guns. The troops stay together in crowded houses. Some sleep outside in tents made from old sails.

Later, 800 Massachusetts troops head to Cambridge. They gather there and then head toward Charlestown. "Where are they going?" you ask an officer.

"Bunker Hill," he replies. "We're going to make the first move—before the British attack Dorchester."

The sound of British cannons wakes you early on June 17, 1775. As the day goes on, more men are sent to Breed's Hill and Bunker Hill. Your regiment will stay in Cambridge.

At the day's end, dirty, bloody men march back to Cambridge. They tell you they didn't have enough ammunition. Many men died, but you know the war has just begun.

THE END

To follow another path, turn to page 121.
To read the conclusion, turn to page 213.

You look at your wife again. You tell your friends you don't want to fight. Your friends look angry. They leave without saying anything.

Soon a larger group comes to the door. "You say you won't fight," one man says. "How do we know you're really a patriot?"

"You could be a Loyalist spy," another says. "If you were one of us, you would have left Boston long before now."

"I'm a patriot," you say. "But my family—"

"We all have families. But we're doing what's right. Maybe you and your family should leave."

The crowd is getting angrier. You fear for your safety. You tell your wife and children to gather whatever they can carry. You leave quickly.

"Go on, coward," someone calls. "Go back to the Loyalists."

Some Loyalists were run out of town by the patriots.

You think Boston is too dangerous now. You decide to stay with relatives in Springfield. The trip will take about 10 days over rough roads, but at least you'll be safe there.

THE END

To follow another path, turn to page 121.
To read the conclusion, turn to page 213.

You decide not to risk leaving Boston. You hope someone else will tell General Ward about the British plans.

On the morning of June 17, you wake early in the morning to the sound of cannons firing. You learn the patriots have built a small fort called a redoubt on Breed's Hill. They worked through the night. British ships have just spotted it now in the daylight.

By noon, you watch the Redcoats gather at the Long Wharf docks. The soldiers climb into boats and begin to cross to Charlestown. Well-dressed Loyalists and other citizens stream by you. They head for the highest hills in the city.

"Where are you going?" you ask a woman.

"To watch the battle. You can see the troops from the hills." Breed's Hill is just a half mile away, and the day is clear. It will be easy to watch the battle.

Turn to page **207**.

Even though you don't like some of the things the king and his government have done in the colonies, you remain loyal to him. You decide to stay in Boston and support the British.

During the next few weeks, food and other supplies run low in Boston. The patriots guard all the roads into the city. They allow very little food to come in. Some Loyalists are able to sneak in food from relatives outside the city. You don't have any relatives who can help. You must pay the high prices charged in the shops.

You can't afford much cheese or bread. For most meals, you eat salted meat and peas.

On June 12, General Gage declares patriots "rebels and traitors." Still, he is willing to pardon any of them who turn in their guns.

A few days later, a British officer comes to you.

"You call yourself a loyal citizen of Great Britain?" he asks.

"Yes sir," you reply. "The patriots are breaking the law."

"Then maybe you can help us. We're asking several Loyalists to go to Cambridge. We want to find out what the patriots are doing."

"You mean you want me to spy?"

"Exactly," the officer says.

You want to help the British defeat the patriots. And if you say no to the officer, he might think you're not truly loyal to the king. But spying is dangerous. If you are caught, the patriots will arrest you—or worse.

To agree to help spy, turn to page **200**.

If you don't want to spy, turn to page **209**.

The officer gives you a pass so you can leave Boston. On the morning of June 16, you walk down Cornhill Street and across Boston Neck. From there, you walk to Cambridge. When you arrive there, you see patriot troops gathering in the center of the city. They wear the same broad hats and simple clothes they wore on their farms. The Redcoats, you think, certainly look more like real soldiers.

You spot a Loyalist you knew in Boston. He fled the city right after the Battles of Lexington and Concord.

"What's going on?" you ask him.

"I'm not sure," he replies. "But it looks like they're getting ready to march somewhere. Perhaps to Charlestown."

"I have to get back to Boston and tell the British," you say.

Patriot troops gathered in Cambridge before heading to Breed's Hill and Bunker Hill.

"It will be faster by boat," the Loyalist says. "I know someone who might be able to help."

The two of you head for the water. On the way, a patriot patrol stops you.

"Where are you two going?" one of the men asks.

Turn the page.

"And who are you?" another demands, sticking his musket into your chest.

"I'm visiting family here in Cambridge," you lie. "I've been staying in Boston to protect our home from the Loyalists."

"Are you sure you're not a Loyalist yourself?" the first man asks. "Maybe even a spy?"

You feel your hands begin to sweat. You could try to lie again, but they might not believe you. Or you could try to run.

To run, go on to page **203**.

To try lying again, turn to page **205**.

You decide to run. You bolt off the road and head into some nearby woods.

"Halt!" the soldiers cry. One of them fires his gun over your head. You keep running, but you don't see a rock in your path. You trip over it and tumble to the ground. Before you can get up again, one of the soldiers is standing above you. His gun is pointed at your chest.

"Not a Loyalist, eh?" he sneers. "You liar. Come on."

The other soldier is guarding your friend. A crowd begins to form as they march you through town.

"What have we here?" someone asks the soldiers. "No-good Loyalists?"

"This one's a spy," the soldier says.

Turn the page.

"Tar and feather them!" another person calls out. You cringe. Just a year before, you watched a mob tear off the clothes of a man cover his body with hot tar and feathers.

"We're bringing them to jail," one of the soldiers says. The guards throw you and your friend into a tiny cell.

The next morning, you hear the distant sound of battle. The patriot troops you had seen yesterday did go to Charlestown, and the British attacked them there.

THE END

To follow another path, turn to page 121.
To read the conclusion, turn to page 213.

You tell the soldier again that you were just here to see your family.

The soldier pokes his gun in your chest and looks you in the eye.

"Alright," he says, "but we'll be watching you. You'd better not be heading back to Boston today."

You and your friend are quite relieved to have been let go. You decide not to risk heading to Boston tonight. You know you will probably not get your information to the British in time. Still, you think you will be safer in Boston with the other Loyalists.

As the sun comes up, you start your walk to Boston. A boat would be faster, but going by land through Roxbury is less risky. It takes you a few hours to walk to Boston.

Turn the page.

As you get nearer to the city, you can hear cannons firing in the harbor. You know the battle has begun. As you enter town, people are still talking about the fort that the patriots built on Breed's Hill. You see lots of townspeople walking toward Beacon Hill. It is a clear day. From the hill, you will be able to watch the battle on Breed's Hill.

Breed's Hill was a half mile from Boston. Citizens climbed on roofs to watch the battle.

You join the crowd of people heading up Beacon Hill. People are climbing onto rooftops. They even sit on the pointed steeples of churches.

The British troops make their way toward a rail fence and stone wall near the redoubt. They move slowly, because the ground in front of them is rocky and covered with tall grass. They carry large packs on their backs.

You know the patriots are waiting behind the fence and wall. The soldiers look like tiny toys, but you know what you're watching is real. The British advance, and the Americans fire. Rows of Redcoats fall to the ground, dead or wounded.

Smoke starts to rise from Charlestown. The town is on fire, most likely set by the British.

Turn the page.

As the fighting goes on, your stomach turns a bit. You never wanted things to come to bloodshed.

Your legs ache. The clock tower at the Old South Meeting House reads just past 4:30. You've been standing on the hill for two hours.

British reinforcements arrive from Charlestown. They are going to make another charge. They storm the redoubt. Soon, you see patriots fleeing the fort on Breed's Hill. A wave of Redcoats chases them off Bunker Hill as well.

By 5:00 in the afternoon, the British have won control of the hills. The battle is over, but the war has just begun.

THE END

To follow another path, turn to page 121.
To read the conclusion, turn to page 213.

"I want to help," you tell the officer, "but I don't want to be a spy. Perhaps I can join the Loyal American Associators."

"We need spies, not guards," he mutters.

You head off to find General Timothy Ruggles, the leader of the Loyal American Associators. He founded the group so Boston Loyalists could help the British defend the city. You can't find Ruggles, but you find one of the officers.

"Here's a musket," he says. "We'll be training tomorrow."

"I thought everyone in the city had turned in their weapons," you say.

"Not us. We can help defend the city if the rebels attack."

Turn the page.

On June 17, General Ruggles meets with the other British generals. They plan their response to a rebel fort built in the night. The British decide to attack the redoubt. You wonder if you will fight too. But when the battle begins that afternoon, you and the other Loyalist militia remain in Boston.

As the day goes on, you see smoke rising from the battlefield and the city of Charlestown. You're told to go to the docks at Long Wharf. Boats are carrying the wounded British soldiers back to Boston. You rush to get your wagon. Soon, the streets around the docks are filled with other wagons, carts, and wheelbarrows. You help carry the wounded. The moans of the injured fill your ears. Your hands are covered with blood.

"Work quickly," one officer says. "We have more boats coming in."

Wounded soldiers were brought to the docks at Long Wharf.

You help pull a wagon of wounded to the hospital. Then you return to the docks for another load. You do this over and over. The boats keep coming all night. Many of the soldiers die. You help bury them in the graveyards around Boston. You hope that the war ends quickly. You don't want anyone digging a grave for you anytime soon.

THE END

To follow another path, turn to page 121.
To read the conclusion, turn to page 213.

The battle on Breed's Hill lasted about two hours.

CHAPTER 5

After the Battle

When the fighting was over on June 17, 1775, the British had won the battle. After the first two British attacks on the redoubt at Breed's Hill, the patriots ran out of ammunition. With their third attack, the Redcoats forced the patriots to flee and retreat to Cambridge.

But the British paid a high price for their victory. They had 226 men killed and 800 other wounded out of 2,200 men. The patriots had just 140 killed and 271 wounded of 1,500 men.

Even with those losses, General Clinton was eager to fight again. He wanted to attack Dorchester within a week, but General Gage refused.

Instead, Gage asked for more troops to defend Boston. After the loss, British generals decided to change their strategy. No more attacks on rebels behind well-built redoubts.

For the Americans, the death of Dr. Joseph Warren was a great loss. Patriots respected his courage and loyalty. There were rumors of his last words. People said Warren told the patriots to "fight on, my brave fellows."

Other stories spread about an order General Putnam gave his troops. He said, "Don't fire until you see the whites of their eyes." Today, many historians think those words are just a legend.

While the Battle of Bunker Hill was going on, patriot leaders formed the Second Continental Congress. They chose George Washington to command the patriot forces.

The next March, Washington placed cannons on Dorchester Heights. Washington knew an attack could destroy Boston. So, he decided to let the British leave the city. By March 17, 1776, the siege of Boston was over.

The Revolutionary War, however, had just begun. In July, the Second Continental Congress approved the Declaration of Independence. The colonists were now fighting for the right to form their own country. The battle for independence lasted for almost seven more years. In 1783, the Americans finally won their independence from the British.

Timeline

October 1768—British troops arrive in Boston to keep order in the city.

December 1773—To protest a tax on tea, patriots throw crates of tea into Boston Harbor; this event is soon called the Boston Tea Party.

April 18, 1775—General Gage sends British troops to Concord, Massachusetts, to seize weapons the patriots have stored there.

April 19, 1775—Patriots and British soldiers fight in Lexington and Concord, marking the start of the Revolutionary War.

April 20, 1775—Thousands of patriot militia from across New England come to the Boston area to prepare for more battles with British soldiers.

May 1775—Patriot leaders from the 13 colonies meet together in Philadelphia at the Second Continental Congress.

June 15, 1775—The patriots learn about British plans to attack Dorchester, south of Boston. Patriots decide they'd rather make the first move and plan an attack from the north.

June 16, 1775—In the cover of night, Colonel William Prescott leads 1,000 men to Charlestown. They are to build a redoubt on Bunker Hill.

June 17, 1775 12:00 a.m.—Patriots decide to build the fort on nearby Breed's Hill instead. They begin digging and building as quietly as possible.

4:00 a.m.—The British awake to see the American activity on Breed's Hill. They begin firing ship cannons and assembling troops.

3:30 p.m.—British soldiers form their lines and begin first attack on the redoubt.

4:00 p.m.—British make a second attempt to take the redoubt.

4:30 p.m.—The British soldiers make a third attack. It is successful. They have won the Battle of Bunker Hill but suffer heavy losses.

March 1776—Patriots bring cannons to Dorchester. British troops withdraw to Nova Scotia. The siege of Boston ends.

September 1783—The Treaty of Paris is signed, officially ending the American Revolution.

Other Paths to Explore

In this book you've seen how the events surrounding the Battle of Bunker Hill look different from three points of view.

Perspectives on history are as varied as the people who lived it. You can explore other paths on your own to learn more about what happened. Seeing history from many points of view is an important part of understanding it.

Here are some ideas for other Revolutionary War points of view to explore:

- King George and the British parliament decided which laws to pass and how to enforce them. What was it like to rule a colony from across the ocean?

- Wives of patriot soldiers had to run farms and businesses without their husbands. What would daily life be like for patriot women?

- Colonists relied on letters, newspapers, and messengers to get information. How would citizens in Boston spread word of the battle? What was it like to be in Philadelphia waiting for news?

The Revolutionary War:

An Interactive History Adventure

By Elizabeth Raum

Consultant:
Len Travers
Associate Professor of History
University of Massachusetts at Dartmouth

Table of Contents

About Your Adventure

YOU live in the American colonies in the late 1700s. Tensions between America and Great Britain are brewing. As war looms on the horizon, which side will you choose?

In this book you'll explore how the choices people made meant the difference between life and death. The events you'll experience happened to real people.

Chapter One sets the scene. Then you choose which path to read. Follow the directions at the bottom of each page. The choices you make will change your outcome. After you finish one path, go back and read the others for new perspectives and more adventures.

YOU CHOOSE the path
you take through history.

Colonists first settled in small towns near the Atlantic Ocean.

CHAPTER 1

War Begins

In 1776, you are living in the American colonies. Like most people in America, you consider yourself British. Some people think of themselves as being from a particular colony, such as Virginia, New York, or Connecticut. You do not feel especially connected to people in the other 12 colonies, though. In fact, like most colonists, you have never traveled more than 30 miles from home.

For the last few years, tensions between the colonies and Britain's King George III have been increasing. When the French and Indian War ended in 1763, Britain was deeply in debt. The king expected the colonists to help pay for Britain's war expenses.

Turn the page.

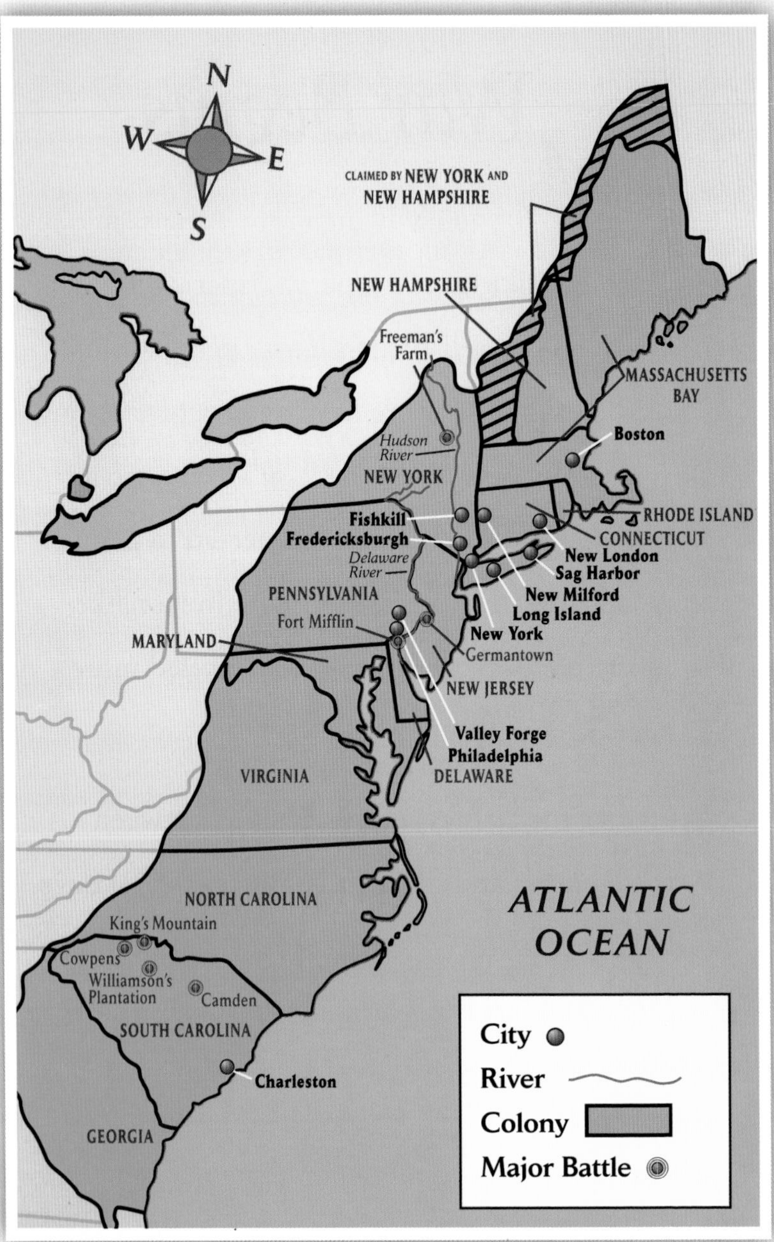
N
S
E
W
CLAIMED BY NEW YORK AND NEW HAMPSHIRE
NEW HAMPSHIRE
Freeman's Farm
MASSACHUSETTS BAY
Boston
Hudson River
NEW YORK
RHODE ISLAND
CONNECTICUT
Fishkill
Fredericksburgh
New London
Sag Harbor
Delaware River
New Milford
PENNSYLVANIA
Long Island
Fort Mifflin
New York
MARYLAND
Germantown
NEW JERSEY
Valley Forge
Philadelphia
DELAWARE
VIRGINIA
ATLANTIC OCEAN
NORTH CAROLINA
King's Mountain
Cowpens
Williamson's Plantation
Camden
SOUTH CAROLINA
Charleston
GEORGIA
City
River
Colony
Major Battle

In 1765 the British government passed the Stamp Act. This law taxed all printed materials, including newspapers, stamps, and playing cards. But Americans objected. They refused to accept laws made by the British parliament.

Great Britain did not back down. Other taxes followed the Stamp Act. In 1768 troops arrived in Boston, Massachusetts, under the leadership of Major General Thomas Gage. Small fights broke out between the soldiers and the townspeople. On March 5, 1770, British soldiers fired into a crowd, killing five men. Patriot leader Samuel Adams called this the Boston Massacre.

On December 16, 1773, colonists dumped British tea in Boston Harbor rather than pay a tax on tea. This was called the Boston Tea Party. In response, Great Britain sent more troops to Massachusetts and closed the port of Boston.

Turn the page.

The other colonies defended Massachusetts. The First Continental Congress, held in Philadelphia in 1774, called on Great Britain to respect the colonists' rights.

On April 19, 1775, American militiamen and British soldiers clashed at Lexington and Concord, Massachusetts. The Americans won these first battles of the Revolutionary War. Great Britain responded by sending more troops to the colonies.

George Washington (on white horse) took charge of the Continental Army in 1775.

British and American troops continued to fight. The British won a major victory at the Battle of Bunker Hill in June 1775.

On July 15, 1775, the Second Continental Congress appointed George Washington commander in chief of the Continental Army. On July 4, 1776, Congress approved the Declaration of Independence.

People throughout the colonies have divided themselves into two groups. Patriots favor independence from Great Britain. Loyalists, also called Tories, want to remain under British rule. The time has come to choose sides. What role will you play in the war?

To be the daughter of a militia captain, turn to page **231**.

To fight as a young Connecticut patriot, turn to page **259**.

To remain loyal to Great Britain, turn to page **293**.

Patriots formed militias, which were groups of citizens ready to fight as soldiers in an emergency.

Daughter of the Revolution

It's October 1776. The war with Britain is underway. In June 1776, the British lost the Battle of Sullivan's Island. Two months later, in August, the British won the Battle of Long Island. Now, British war ships are gathering off the coast of New York. More fighting seems likely.

Soldiers, traders, and supplies pass through your hometown of Fredericksburgh, New York, daily. One day, your brother Robert runs into the house. "Someone's coming," he shouts.

You rush outside as a man on horseback comes into the yard. "I've come from Fishkill with a message," he says.

Turn the page.

"Follow me," you say. You lead the way to the gristmill where your father is grinding grain into flour. Father heads the local militia regiment.

After the messenger leaves, Father says, "The militia must to go to Fishkill and guard the Hudson River."

You help pack food and supplies. Wives often go to war with their husbands, but your mother has a new baby. She cannot travel. You offer to go along. "I'm 15. I can cook and clean for you."

"You may come if you want," Father says. "But there is important work here too. Enoch Crosby, the shoemaker, is one of our spies. His information helps us fight the British. He may need help."

To go to Fishkill with Father, go to page **233**.

To stay home, turn to page **235**.

You go with Father to Fishkill. The town is headquarters for John Jay and his Committee of Safety. The committee provides leadership in the struggle for independence.

You and Father rent rooms above Mrs. Mary Bloodgood's hat shop. A few days later, Father goes to the town of White Plains. It is about 50 miles south of Fishkill. "General Washington fears there will be a British attack there," he says.

While Father is away, you stay with Mrs. Bloodgood. Father returns to Fishkill on November 4. He tells you about the Battle of White Plains. "On October 28, we fired some shots at the British. They fired back," Father says. "We thought they'd come after us, but they didn't. They marched back to New York City."

Turn the page.

"Did you meet General Washington?" you ask.

"Yes. He's a great leader," Father says. "When he speaks, men listen."

Militiamen serve for a few months at a time. By winter, you and Father go home. It's good to be with the family again. But in September 1777, you return with Father to Fishkill. General Washington orders patriots to go north and stop British General John Burgoyne and his troops. Mrs. Bloodgood suggests that Father let you stay with her. "The fighting could be heavy," she says.

To go home to Fredericksburgh, go to page **235**.

To go north with the militia, turn to page **242**.

To stay at Fishkill, turn to page **244**.

There's plenty to do on the farm and at your father's gristmill. Weeks and months pass quickly. You receive word that General Washington is in New Jersey. Father remains in Fishkill to guard supplies there.

One night, there's a knock at the door. It's late. You are in bed. The rest of the family is already asleep. It could be Crosby or another patriot needing help. Or it could be British soldiers.

To answer the door, turn to page **236**.

To go wake Mother, turn to page **237**.

You answer the door. It's Enoch Crosby, the patriot spy. "Quick, hide me," he whispers. "British soldiers are following me."

You want to help Crosby, but if the British find a spy in your house, they might burn it down. Maybe you should send Crosby out the back door. He can hide in the barn or the gristmill, unless the soldiers are covering the back too.

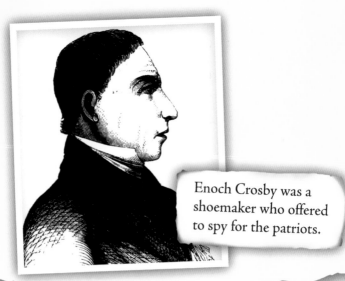

Enoch Crosby was a shoemaker who offered to spy for the patriots.

To show Crosby out the back door, turn to page **247**.

To hide him in the house, turn to page **249**.

You go upstairs to wake Mother, but the knocking stops. Whoever was there goes away.

A few nights later, someone knocks again. "We're the king's soldiers, and we're hungry!" they shout.

Your mother comes down the stairs. "If we don't open the door, they'll knock it down," she says.

You and your mother prepare bread and cheese for the British soldiers. "Soon we'll be eating like this every day," one soldier says.

Another soldier gives him a nudge. "Watch what you say."

"These women are no danger to the British! Neither are the rebels at Fishkill. We'll have no trouble at all," his friend says.

Turn the page.

It's after midnight when the soldiers leave.

"They plan to attack the supply depot at Fishkill," you tell your mother.

"Yes, I believe you're right," she says.

"I must find a way to warn Father."

But your mother warns you, "The woods are full of Cow Boys and Skinners."

Cow Boys and Skinners are dangerous men who often hide in the woods. Cow Boys steal supplies for the British. Skinners favor the patriots, but if they're hungry, they'll steal from anyone. Neither will stop to ask who you are. "Contact the spy network instead," Mother pleads.

To go to Fishkill to find Father, go to page **239**.

To contact the spy network operating in the area, turn to page **250**.

The sooner you tell Father, the better. It's a 20-mile trip through thick forests. It's late, and you have only the moon to light your way.

You saddle your horse, Blaze, and leave home. You hope the darkness will hide you from the Cow Boys and Skinners. You push Blaze to run faster.

Something smacks you in the head. It's a tree branch. You fly off Blaze. Before you can move, a boot lands on your stomach. "Stop! You're hurting me!" you cry. You grab the man's boot and twist it hard.

"Ouch!" he yells. You keep twisting until he loses his balance and falls. You leap up, run to Blaze, and race into the night. You're safe for now, but badly frightened.

To continue to Fishkill, turn to page **240**.

To circle around and go home, turn to page **250**.

You race on. The sun is rising as you arrive in Fishkill. You find your father with John Jay.

"Is something wrong at home?" Father asks.

"Everyone is fine," you reply. You warn him about the British attack.

"Good work," Jay tells you.

Father is staying in the room over Mary Bloodgood's hat shop. She offers you breakfast.

"I don't want you going home alone. It's too dangerous," Father says after you tell him about the man in the woods. "I must go north with the militia tomorrow. British General John Burgoyne is marching his troops south. If another British general, General Howe, marches north from New York City, the British will control the route up the Hudson River to Canada. They are trying to separate New England from the rest of the colonies. We must stop him."

John Jay was a member of the Continental Congress.

"Then I'll go north with you," you say.

"Or you could stay here with me," Mrs. Bloodgood offers. "You'll be safer, and I can use the help."

To go north with Father, turn to page **242**.

To stay in Fishkill, turn to page **244**.

You're eager to go north with the militia. Perhaps you can help. You walk behind the supply wagons with other women and children.

"What would the army do without us women?" one woman says. "We sew, cook, do laundry, and care for the sick and wounded. I've even seen women pick up a gun during battle and shoot."

General Washington has sent militia to guard the Hudson River from Burgoyne's troops. On September 18, 1777, you camp at Freeman's Farm on the Hudson River. Scouts report that the British are camped 2 miles away.

The next morning, Colonel Daniel Morgan and his Virginia riflemen are first onto the battlefield. Other militia groups join them. You wait with the women behind the troops. It's quiet, almost eerie.

First you hear a single shot, then hundreds follow. Noise and smoke fill the air. Suddenly a soldier stumbles out of the smoke. "Help me," he calls. Blood gushes from a wound on his right arm. You rush forward and press a cloth against the wound. The bleeding slows.

Another soldier calls out, and another. You fill a bucket with water and head toward the voices.

Before you realize it, you are in the midst of the fighting. A soldier lies on the ground, bleeding. Nearby, a group of soldiers are firing a large cannon.

"Give us a hand here," a soldier calls. "We need water to cool down the cannon."

To continue tending the wounded, turn to page **245**.

To help cool the cannon, turn to page **255**.

"I'm glad you decided to stay," Mrs. Bloodgood says. "One of the biggest needs is clothing," she explains. "You can help by sewing and washing clothes with Mrs. Woodhull. She's in charge of clothing supplies. Or you can help at the hospital. Nursing is difficult but important work."

To sew clothes, turn to page **251**.

To work as a nurse, turn to page **253**.

Someone else will have to get water. You want to help the fallen soldier. You press a cloth against his wounded arm to stop the bleeding. Then you tie a bandage around his arm.

Other soldiers call for help. Many men have gaping gunshot wounds. Others have been pierced by British bayonets.

You hold the hands of the dying. Then you move on to help others. One man cries out for his mother. You give what comfort you can. He dies with his head resting in your lap.

The fighting lasts for five hours. By the end of the day, blood soaks your dress. Smoke and tears smear your face. Soldiers carry the wounded to a medical tent and bury the dead.

"We won the battle," a doctor says. "But we lost 80 men."

Turn the page.

Some women helped wounded soldiers on the battlefields.

More than 200 Americans were wounded in the battle. Most of the wounded soldiers will be moved to a hospital in Fishkill.

"We need nurses to care for the soldiers there. Would you help?" the doctor asks.

You don't want to return to the battlefield. But nursing is such sad work. Perhaps you could help repair uniforms instead.

To repair uniforms, turn to page **251**.

To work at the hospital, turn to page **253**.

You don't dare hide Crosby inside the house. "Follow me," you say, checking to see that the way is clear. You lead Crosby to the mill. Once inside, you duck behind bags of flour. It should be safe here.

You hear a crashing noise. Soldiers are in the mill!

"Take this flour," one man yells. "We may not have found the spy, but at least we found supplies." The soldiers haul bag after bag of flour out of the mill into a waiting wagon. You signal to Crosby to follow you out the side door. Maybe you can escape before the soldiers notice you.

"Stop!"

They've seen you. Two men grab you, and three take hold of Crosby.

Turn the page.

"What are you doing?" Crosby says. "Can't a man visit his girl? I just wanted to say good-bye before I leave to serve for the British."

"British?" they ask.

Crosby is a very convincing liar. The men believe him. "You're welcome to the flour," Crosby says, "but there's no need to frighten a young girl." They let you go.

Once the soldiers are gone, Crosby leaves. "I'll be back," he says with a smile. "Thank you for giving me a safe place to hide."

Turn to page **257.**

Crosby can hide in the house. There's a secret staircase that leads to the attic. He slips upstairs into the darkness. You blow out the candles and rush back to your bed.

Suddenly you hear more knocking. The baby cries. You, Mother, and all the other children get up. They crowd around her as she opens the door.

Two British soldiers stand there. "Sorry to bother you. But we are looking for a troublemaker."

"No one has come by here," Mother says, trying to calm the crying baby. "We were all asleep."

As soon as they leave, you tell Mother that Crosby is hiding in the attic. She smiles. "Your father will be pleased. Keep Crosby hidden until the soldiers are far away."

The next night, Crosby sneaks away to deliver his secrets to John Jay and the Committee of Safety.

Turn to page **257**.

The woods are too dangerous. The message will have to wait.

The next morning, you go to town. Mrs. Clark, who runs a small bookshop, is a trusted friend of liberty.

"Have you seen Crosby lately?" you whisper.

She takes you into the back of the store. "I can reach him." She agrees to relay your message to Crosby. "He'll get it to John Jay."

"You're one of us now," she says. You're proud that you've found a way to help win freedom.

THE END

To follow another path, turn to page 229.
To read the conclusion, turn to page 319.

You decide to repair uniforms with Mrs. Woodhull, who is in charge of the clothing supplies. "Women throughout the colonies are sewing," she says. "In Connecticut, every town has a quota of clothing they must provide to us here in Fishkill. In Hartford, for example, the women are to complete 1,000 coats and 1,600 shirts. People in other colonies are helping too."

Everything is sewn by hand. You sew all day. Then you sew by candlelight until you fall asleep.

In October Father returns to Fishkill. "Britain's General Burgoyne surrendered at the Battle of Saratoga," he says. "I'm free to go home."

"May I stay at Fishkill to sew with Mrs. Woodhull?" you ask.

"Of course," he replies.

Turn the page.

As the war goes on, the Continental Army runs out of warm coats, pants, and socks. They are out of shoes too, but you can't sew shoes.

By 1778 there's a building at Fishkill just for men who have no clothing at all. Their shirts, pants, and socks wore out, and they have no others. They cannot return to war service without clothes. Every outfit you complete means one soldier returns to battle. Some patriots fight the British with guns and rifles. You win freedom with a sewing needle.

THE END

To follow another path, turn to page 229.
To read the conclusion, turn to page 319.

Fishkill's Trinity Church was used as a hospital during the Revolutionary War.

Trinity Church becomes the hospital. Pews are moved out and cots moved in. The wounded soldiers are brought back to Fishkill.

There are hundreds of soldiers in the hospital. Many are terribly wounded. Caring for them is hard work.

Turn the page.

You help prepare the men's meals and try to make them comfortable. You wash their bodies, change bandages, and give medicine. Occasionally you help doctors remove wounded arms or legs.

Often you write letters to wives, mothers, and girlfriends. Many soldiers are too badly wounded to write themselves. They mumble the words as you write. Others don't know how to read or write. Thanks to you, their families will learn what happened. Some soldiers will live to return home, but their wounds will change their lives forever. You will always remember the patriots who gave their lives to win the war.

THE END

To follow another path, turn to page 229.
To read the conclusion, turn to page 319.

You rush to the cannon. The soldier grabs your pail of water. He dips a sponge in the water and uses it to cool the cannon. The cannon must be cooled each time it fires 10 or 12 rounds.

After the battle ends, you gather up rifles and muskets left behind on the battlefield. General Washington's troops are short of weapons, and a good musket costs more than a week's pay.

During battles, soldiers used water to keep their cannons cool.

Turn the page.

On October 17, 1777, General Burgoyne surrenders at the Battle of Saratoga. Defeating Burgoyne is a good sign for the Americans. Your father's regiment returns home. He'll go off again, but next time you'll stay home to help Mother with the farm. You were a good soldier, but you're needed more at home.

THE END

To follow another path, turn to page 229.
To read the conclusion, turn to page 319.

That's not the last you see of Enoch Crosby. Throughout the war, he sends secret information about British troop movements to the patriots. He relies on you to provide him with a hiding place. You create a special code. Now you recognize Crosby's knock.

Sometimes you even carry messages from Crosby to Mrs. Clark, who runs a small bookshop in town. She's part of the spy network too. You keep secrets during the war. Years later you tell your grandchildren that you helped win the American War of Independence.

THE END

To follow another path, turn to page 229.
To read the conclusion, turn to page 319.

Many young men signed up for the adventure of fighting on a privateer.

Patriot Courage

It is the spring of 1777. It seems as if all the young men in New Milford, Connecticut, are going to war. Many stop by your father's farm to say good-bye. One friend tells you he's going to sea on a privateer. "Privateers hunt and capture British ships," he says. "Lots of our own merchant ships have become privateers. I've already signed on with one. You could find a place too."

You're tempted. You were only 14 when the war began in 1775, but now you are 16. You ask Father for permission to go to war.

He can see the determination in your eyes. He hesitates, but then he shakes his head.

Turn the page.

"A sailor's life is not easy. The work is dangerous. It's no life for a farmer like you," Father says.

The next day, you go into New Milford for farm supplies. Some men at the general store tell you that the town is being divided into squads. Each squad must provide a soldier for the Continental Army. Many men refuse because they have wives and children to support. Others are too old.

A group of rich storeowners offers you money if you will serve for them. Your father could use the money to hire someone to take your place. But going to sea sounds more exciting.

To join the Continental Army, go to page **261**.

To go to sea on a privateer, turn to page **264**.

You take the money. It will help your family. You join the 8th Connecticut Regiment at Newtown, Connecticut. An officer leads you and the other recruits to Peekskill, New York, on the Hudson River. Peekskill is a major supply depot.

You spend the summer guarding the supplies and learning how to load a musket quickly. Between each shot, you pour gunpowder into the barrel. You then put a lead ball in the muzzle and shove it down. You put some gunpowder on the pan of the musket and pull back the hammer. It's ready to fire again.

"If you train hard," the captain says, "you'll get off three shots a minute."

Turn the page.

In early September your regiment leaves for Pennsylvania. "The British have taken Philadelphia," your captain announces. "We'll go on to Germantown, Pennsylvania."

On October 4, the captain orders your unit to form a line. "Today we fight. The British are just ahead. Don't fire until you see the buttons upon their clothes!" the captain orders.

But the British begin firing before you are that close. Once the guns and cannons go off, all you see is smoke and fire. Your regiment moves forward. You fire, reload, and fire again, not knowing whether your bullets reach their marks.

Your army pushes the British troops back through their own camp. Then you and your fellow soldiers begin to run out of gunpowder.

The British renew their attack. They shoot at you and charge with their bayonets.

Everyone in your regiment is retreating. You've got no choice but to join them. Amid the noise and shouting, you lose your sense of direction. The grove of trees to the left looks familiar. You head there.

By the time you realize you've turned the wrong way, it's too late. You are face-to-face with a young British soldier. He looks as scared as you are. His gun is aimed at you. Yours is aimed at him. If you shoot, neither of you will miss. You have to think fast.

To fire your musket, turn to page **269**.

To distract the soldier, turn to page **270**.

To surrender, turn to page **274**.

You travel to Bedford Village, Massachusetts. You have an uncle there. It's good to see him. You enjoy a good meal, a good night's sleep, and then you go to the docks. You find Captain Mowry Potter aboard the *Eagle*.

"What do you want?" he asks.

"I'm looking for work on a privateer," you say.

"I'm looking for a cabin boy," he offers.

"But I'm 16, and I want to be a sailor," you say.

"You may be 16, but you're a small fellow. Start as a cabin boy. You need to learn the ropes."

Soon the *Eagle* sets sail. Potter is a harsh master, and the sailors are rough. They take the best of the food and leave the scraps for you. You try to do as the captain asks, but he's quick to scold you for the slightest mistake.

Privateers helped the American Navy battle the British at sea.

Captain Potter cruises along the British coast, looking for British ships. But you don't see a single one. In October 1777, the *Eagle* begins its return journey to Massachusetts.

One day, you spot a tall pole standing alone on the horizon. "Is that land?" you ask an officer.

"Looks more like the bare poles of a ship," he says. He peers through his spyglass. "It's flying a British flag, and it's raising its sails."

Turn the page.

"They are chasing us. Faster, faster!" Captain Potter yells, but you can't get away. In half an hour, the British warship *Sphynx* catches up with the *Eagle*. Its 20 huge guns are aimed at the hull.

"We are taken," a sailor says, hanging his head. "We're as good as dead."

Captain Hunt of the *Sphynx* sends small boats to the *Eagle*. You climb into a boat that takes you back to the British ship. There, sailors toss you a rope. You tie it around your chest so they can haul you up to the ship. Once everyone is aboard the *Sphynx*, the British sink the *Eagle*.

"What a waste," you say.

"If we didn't sink it, we would have burned it," a British sailor says. "We don't need any more supplies."

He notices the buttons on your shirt. They are made of pewter. The motto "Liberty and Property" is engraved on them. "Yankee!" he says with a sneer. He pulls out a knife to snip the buttons away.

"Leave him alone. He's just a boy," a passing British officer growls. You're surprised. The British sailors are kinder to you than the men on the *Eagle*.

The *Sphynx* goes directly to New York, which is under British control. There, the crew from the *Eagle* is sent to the *Asia,* a British prison ship. Supper is a bit of moldy bread and watery soup. There aren't any beds. You sleep on the hard deck wherever you can find room.

One day, some prisoners try to escape by jumping overboard. Two are shot in the water by British guards, but the others make it safely ashore. Their escape gives you hope. You begin to plan your own escape.

Turn the page.

A few days later, a British officer boards the ship. He is looking for a cabin boy for his ship, the *Maidstone*. "You," he says, pointing to a boy named Paul.

But Paul doesn't want to leave his father, who is also a prisoner on the *Asia*. Paul cries and screams. He puts up such a fuss that the officer lets him go.

The officer turns to you. "Do you want to stay here too? The food is better on the *Maidstone*."

To go with the officer to the Maidstone,
turn to page **271**.

To stay onboard the Asia *and try to escape,*
turn to page **275**.

You fire your musket first. The soldier falls, blood gushing from his head. You fall to your knees and vomit. You've killed a man. You'll have to live with this your entire life — if you survive the war.

You listen. Off to the right, there are voices. They sound familiar. That's the direction you should have gone in the first place. You stand up, wipe your mouth, and run toward the voices.

Turn to page **276**.

"Look!" you say, pointing to a distant tree. It's an old trick, but it works. The soldier looks away. You rush forward and knock the musket from his hands. Then you push him down. You're tempted to shoot him, but you resist. The blast might alert his fellow soldiers. You kick him in the stomach. He yelps in pain. Suddenly you hear voices coming from the woods. They sound familiar. You dash in their direction.

Turn to page **276**.

You go to the *Maidstone* with the officer, Mr. Richards. You cook his meals and clean his clothes and cabin for him. The *Maidstone* cruises the American coast as far south as Virginia, capturing merchant vessels and sailors. In Virginia, the *Maidstone* captures ships full of tobacco. The money from selling the tobacco will be split among the crew. Even you will get a share.

In December 1777, the *Maidstone* comes alongside a passing British ship. Mr. Richards leans over the rail. "Any news of the war?" he shouts.

Turn the page.

"Burgoyne surrendered at Saratoga in October. The Americans have taken thousands of his men prisoner," a man on the other ship yells.

Burgoyne? No one can believe it. He is one of Great Britain's best generals. His men are highly trained British soldiers.

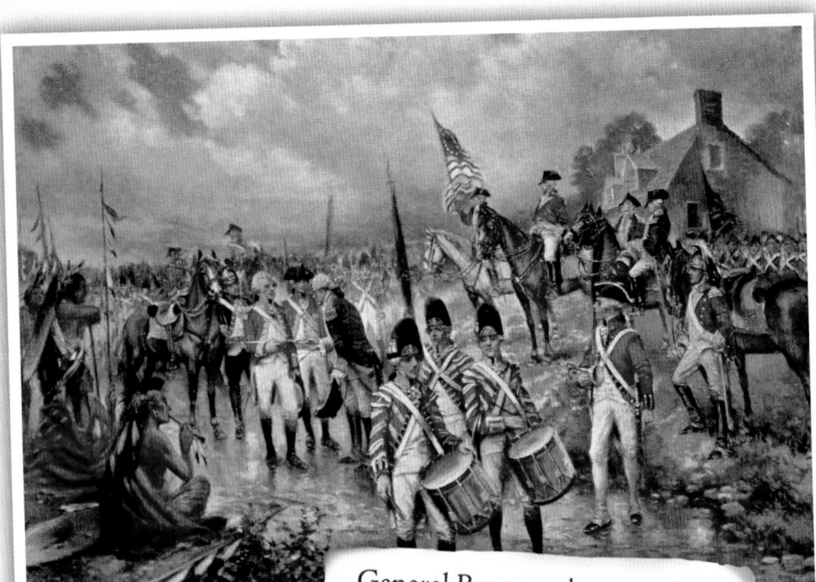

General Burgoyne's surrender at Saratoga was a turning point in the war.

One spring day while the ship is in New York Harbor, you are allowed to go onshore. It's your first time onshore since you left home. Knowing you are watched, you make no attempt to escape.

Several days later, Mr. Richards sends you ashore again with his laundry. You walk about the city. This time, no one is watching. There's a milk boat at the dock.

The captain of the milk boat is friendly. He has just made a delivery and is returning to Long Island.

"My uncle lives there," you say.

He offers you a ride. "But the British control Long Island. If you're not careful, you'll end up fighting for the British. Or you'll end up dead."

To go to Long Island, turn to page **282**.

To return to the ship, turn to page **284**.

You lift your hands in surrender. "I give up," you say. You refuse to shoot a man at such close range. You're a soldier, not a murderer.

The soldier takes you to the British camp. A few days later, the British march their prisoners to the coast. There, you are put on the prison ship *Asia*. There are hundreds of other patriot soldiers and sailors onboard. The ship begins its journey to New York Harbor.

Every morning, the officer shouts, "Rebels, turn out your dead!" One day, you notice the man sleeping next to you has not moved. You nudge him. He's dead! He either starved or died of disease.

If you're going to survive, you'll have to escape. One dark night, a thunderstorm provides the perfect cover. You wait until a clap of thunder distracts the guards. Then you jump into the icy water of New York's East River and swim. You wait for gunshots, but nothing happens.

You spy a small fishing boat in the distance. It's a long way to shore, and you are not a strong swimmer. The boat is closer. But are the fishermen patriots or Loyalists?

To swim for shore, turn to page **281**.

To head to the boat, turn to page **283**.

The voices were men from your regiment. You join them on the march toward Philadelphia. "We almost won the Battle of Germantown," one of the men says. "If only we hadn't run out of ammunition . . ." You know that's hopeful thinking. You were outnumbered by the British.

Your regiment marches on without stopping. At last you reach White Marsh, 12 miles north of Philadelphia. You sleep on the soft ground. It's dirtier than a pigsty, and the smoke from the campfires burns your eyes. Supply wagons deliver beef. The cooks roast it over the fire. Your small share is burnt on the outside and raw inside, but you gobble it up eagerly.

One day your captain announces, "General Washington has ordered us to defend the forts on the Delaware River south of Philadelphia. We'll camp at Fort Mifflin and keep the British ships from coming up the river."

You march on toward Fort Mifflin. You spend the first night in a village where the people offer you a good meal and a warm bed. But the next day, you go hungry again. On the third day, you find a goose. By the time it is cooked and divided up, you get one wing. There's no salt or bread to go with it.

In late October 1777, you reach Fort Mifflin. You set up camp and take turns standing guard. An officer takes you aside. "This could be rough," he says. "There are 400 of us trying to hold back the entire British Navy."

A zigzag stone wall makes up one side of the fort. The other sides are half-built stone walls separated by ditches. Cannons line the walls. A small pen between a stone wall and one of the fort's wooden walls is the only safe place.

Turn the page.

More than 150 Continental soldiers died in the Battle of Fort Mifflin.

For five weeks, 12 British ships fire on the fort. The British lob more than 10,000 cannonballs over the fort's walls. After so much bombing, the fort's walls are rubble. There is no protection left.

"We must raise a signal flag to the American ships in the river to the north. They will help us," an officer shouts. He asks for volunteers to raise the flag.

Before you can offer your help, a sergeant volunteers. He climbs to the top of the flagpole and attaches the flag. But as he climbs down, he is hit by British gunfire. He falls to his death.

Soon four or five American ships begin firing on the British. Their help gives you some relief, but it's not enough. The British have won the battle.

That night, you and the rest of the soldiers sneak away. Before you leave, you take one last look at the fort. The area looks as empty as a plowed field.

You have served in the Continental Army long enough. It's time to go home. But your captain urges you to be a good patriot and sign up for another year.

To go home, turn to page **280.**

To stay in the Continental Army, turn to page **286.**

You're eager to return to Connecticut. It's a long walk through British territory. One day you pass a farmhouse. You steal six eggs from the barn and grab a shirt and pants off the clothesline. You feel rich! You're not only warmer, but now you look like a farmer, not a soldier.

When you reach New York City, you go to the docks. One of the boats carries milk from Long Island to the city. You tell the captain that your uncle lives on Long Island.

"Would you like a ride?" he offers. If you can reach Sag Harbor, your uncle will help you get home. But it is dangerous. Long Island is also a British stronghold.

To go to Long Island, turn to page **282.**

To keep walking, turn to page **285.**

You swim to shore. By the time you reach the river's edge, you are exhausted and shivering. There's a man in the distance. "Hello there!" you call. Then you realize that the man is wearing the red coat of a British soldier. He takes you back to the *Asia*.

"Give him 20 lashes," the commander says.

You are tied to a mast, and your bare back is whipped. The whip slashes stripes in your back. Blood runs onto the deck.

Friends drag you away, wipe the blood off your back, and give you water. But you develop an infection and a high fever. Nothing helps. You die a few days later, and your body is dumped overboard.

THE END

To follow another path, turn to page 229.
To read the conclusion, turn to page 319.

You take the ride to Long Island. It's a long walk to Sag Harbor where your uncle lives. You walk all day. When darkness falls, you find an empty barn and sleep in the hay. Your stomach aches from hunger.

The next morning, an old woman gets water from the well near the barn. Then she goes back to the house. Should you ask her for food? If she's a patriot, she'll help you. If she's loyal to the British, she might turn you in.

To ask for food, turn to page **289**.

To keep moving, turn to page **291**.

Brrr! The cold makes you weak. You head for the boat. "Hello there!" you call, and someone drops a rope into the water.

An old fisherman pulls you aboard. "Where are you headed?" he asks.

"I've got an uncle in Sag Harbor on Long Island," you say.

You stay with the fisherman and his wife for a week. When you are strong enough, you thank them and begin walking. Your uncle's house is 110 miles away. You walk by day and sleep in fields at night. By the third day, you are out of food. You see a farmhouse. You spend the night in the nearby barn. The next day, you're starving. Should you knock on the farmhouse door and ask for food?

To ask for food, turn to page **289**.

To pass by, turn to page **291**.

You return to the *Maidstone*. Why risk your life? Mr. Richards has been good to you. You spend the rest of the war on the ship. The officers treat you fairly. The American privateers you've met are far rougher than the British sailors. You've come to believe that the colonists would be better off under British rule.

When the war ends, the Americans gain independence. But you decide to remain on a British ship as a British sailor. You feel more at home on ship than you do on land. And you feel more British than American.

THE END

To follow another path, turn to page 229.
To read the conclusion, turn to page 319.

It's safer to walk, so you keep going. At night, you sleep in barns. You take a fresh shirt and a pair of pants from a clothesline. You rip up a sheet and wrap it around your bare, bleeding feet. Your stomach growls with hunger. You've had nothing to eat but a few chestnuts.

At last you reach familiar country. Now you can safely ask for help. Neighbors welcome you back and give you food, clothing, and a ride home. What joy! You've served your time with the Continental Army. From now until America wins freedom in 1783, you serve in the Connecticut militia. You're ready to defend nearby villages and farms if the British attack.

THE END

To follow another path, turn to page 229.
To read the conclusion, turn to page 319.

"I'm a true son of liberty," you say. "I'll stay in the army until the war ends or until I die trying to win it."

A few days before Christmas 1777, you reach Valley Forge in Pennsylvania. General Washington is camped here. You see him walking through camp in his blue uniform. He towers over the other officers. His face is grim.

George Washington was in charge of the troops at Valley Forge.

An officer calls the soldiers together. "We're to begin building huts for winter housing," he says. "General Washington has offered $1 each to the men who finish their hut first."

There are 12 men in your unit. Building a hut without tools is a challenge, but you finish it in two days. You win $1 each!

Now you have a hut, but no blankets, clothes, or shoes. You have a few stools, but the only bedding is straw tossed on the cold, dirt floor.

You don't have much to eat. Most of the time, you live on fire cake. It's made by adding a bit of water to flour and then grilling it over a hot fire.

Your shoes are worn out. On guard duty, you stand on your hat to protect your bare feet. Even so, they bleed and ache from the cold.

Turn the page.

Snow makes travel impossible, but still the soldiers threaten to leave. At night, the chant begins in one hut and travels to the next and the next. "No meat, no coat, no flour, no soldier." Each day you grow thinner.

You wake one morning in February 1778 feeling hot. Has the weather changed? No, you have a fever. Your friends bring you water, but there is nothing else to offer. Your fever grows worse. First you have chills. Then your skin feels like it's on fire. You develop a cough.

"Influenza," the doctor says. "We have no medicine. Keep him warm. Give him water."

But it's not enough. You survived British cannons, but you don't survive the flu.

THE END

To follow another path, turn to page 229.
To read the conclusion, turn to page 319.

You knock on the door and ask for something to eat. "You're not a rebel, are you?" an old woman asks.

"I'm loyal to King George," you lie.

"In that case," she says, "you are welcome to join me for Johnnycakes." She places three of the flattened cornmeal cakes onto a tin plate for you.

As you finish eating, three British soldiers stop by. They look at your empty plate. "Are you feeding rebels too?" they ask the woman.

"Never, sir," she says. "He's as loyal to King George as you are."

"Aye," you say. "It's true. But I must be on my way." They let you go. It was a close call!

Turn the page.

Eventually you find Uncle's house in Sag Harbor. After a few weeks, your uncle arranges for you to take a boat across Long Island Sound to Connecticut under cover of darkness.

It's great to be home. You join the local militia. Your days of fighting with the main army are over. But you help the militia defend Connecticut against several British raids. In that way, you continue to help America win independence in 1783.

THE END

To follow another path, turn to page 229.
To read the conclusion, turn to page 319.

It's safer not to ask. You sneak out of the barn. As you walk, a farmer driving a wagonload of hay pulls up behind you. "Need a ride?" he asks. You hop aboard. When he asks where you are going, you mention your uncle's name.

"He's a good man, a real patriot," the farmer says. He takes you directly to Uncle's house. After a few days, Uncle pays your fare on a boat traveling across Long Island Sound to Connecticut. Your parents are thrilled to have you safely home. "You'll stay?" Father asks.

"Yes," you say. You join the Connecticut militia. If the British attack nearby villages, you're ready and willing to fight. Until then, you work the farm with Father. It feels good to be home.

THE END

To follow another path, turn to page 229.
To read the conclusion, turn to page 319.

British soldiers cut off supplies to the city of Charleston, South Carolina, until the Americans surrendered.

Young Loyalist

It's May 12, 1780, and you live on a plantation near Charleston, South Carolina. Your family is celebrating the surrender of Charleston to the British. In early April, the British began firing on the city. The city was under siege.

On May 11, British General Henry Clinton's guns set fire to several homes. American commander General Benjamin Lincoln and his force of about 5,000 Continental soldiers fought bravely. But the British force was larger and better equipped. Today Lincoln surrendered. The battle for Charleston is over.

Turn the page.

Father is pleased. He's a Loyalist who favors Great Britain. He admires British wealth and power. "They can protect our coastline from outside attack, and they will stop the threat from the Cherokee Indians on the frontier," he says.

"You could go to Charleston," Father says. "It's safely in British hands. And your uncle needs help with his shipping business."

"But I like it here at the plantation," you answer.

"The choice is yours," Father says.

To stay on the plantation, go to page **295.**

To go to Charleston, turn to page **302.**

"I'll stay on the plantation," you say. Your jobs include caring for the horses and checking on the 30 slaves who work on the plantation. When you arrive home from church one Sunday, three slaves are missing.

"I promised not to tell, but they've gone to join the British troops," your little sister says. "They say that any slave who fights for the British can earn his freedom."

"We need those workers," Father says. "When did they leave?"

"Last night."

"It's too late to catch up to them," you say. "Just let them go."

"I hate to do that," Father tells you.

To go after the slaves, turn to page **296.**

To let them go, turn to page **297.**

You go after the slaves. If you can find them, your father will be pleased with you. You follow a path through the swamp.

Suddenly, someone tosses a net over your head. A gruff voice says, "Caught you, you stinking Loyalist!" You recognize the men as rebels who own small farms nearby. Since the loss of Charleston, rebels hide in the woods. They steal supplies from local farms and attack Loyalists like you and Father.

The rebels tie your arms and drag you to their camp. "We'll teach you a lesson," they say.

"Wait!" one of the men says. "This boy may not share his father's views. Are you a patriot? Or are you loyal to King George?"

To say you are a patriot, turn to page **298**.

To tell the truth, turn to page **299**.

Father finally agrees to let the slaves go. "Perhaps they'll return," he says. "For now, the remaining slaves will have to work harder."

A few days pass. You are working in the barn when your sister comes running. "Four strange men are approaching," she says. "Come quickly!"

You race to the house. Your father and brother have gone to town for supplies. "Be calm," you say to Mother. "Give them food, and they'll go away."

"Take the silver and bury it in the swamp. These men look like thieves," Mother says.

"It's too late," you tell mother. "We'll hide the silver in the attic."

"No, they'll be sure to look there," Mother says. "Please, hide it in the swamp."

To hide the silver in the swamp, turn to page **304**.

To hide it in the attic, turn to page **309**.

"I'm a patriot," you lie. "I'll help you."

The men believe you and cut you loose. They tell you that they are part of a militia regiment. They want to prevent the British from winning the rest of South Carolina.

The men plan to raid a nearby plantation for supplies in the morning. You don't want any part of it. You will need to sneak away from them.

You wait until the forest grows dark. When the men fall asleep, you tiptoe away.

Turn to page **300**.

It's tempting to lie, but you tell the truth. "My father's a good man," you say. "If he supports King George, then so do I."

"Well, then you had better pray that King George will save you before morning."

The men laugh and drink their rum. Soon they are snoring beside the campfire. This is the moment you've been waiting for! You work your arms free and sneak away.

Rebels often hid in the woods and attacked passing Loyalists.

You don't dare go home in case the men come after you. You steal a horse and set out for Camden, about 120 miles north of Charleston. One of Father's friends, Colonel Zacharias Gibbs, owns a plantation there.

Gibbs is a Loyalist hero. He was captured at the Battle of Kettle Creek in Georgia in 1779. He spent 15 months in a prison run by rebels.

It takes nearly a week to reach Gibbs' home. He welcomes you and asks about Father. You explain what has happened.

"We need men like you fighting to keep this country loyal to Britain," he says.

"I've been thinking of joining the South Carolina Royalists," you say. The colonel nods approvingly. But later, he tells you more about his time in battle and in prison. You realize you might be safer going to Charleston to help your uncle, like your father had suggested.

To go to Charleston, turn to page **302**.

To join the South Carolina Royalists, turn to page **306**.

"Welcome to Charleston," Uncle says. He is a clever businessman who does business with both Loyalists and patriots. Now that the British are in control, business booms. Your uncle signs a note of congratulations to Great Britain's General Clinton. So do 206 others. "That could be dangerous if the British lose this war," you say.

"Don't talk nonsense," Uncle says. "The British won't lose. They have the best-trained army in the world. Their victory here in Charleston is the turning point in this war."

You sign an Oath of Allegiance to the Crown. The oath provides British protection for anyone who signs. Even some patriots sign the oath.

"Don't trust anyone," Uncle warns. "Some people in Charleston are taking supplies to the rebels in the countryside. Watch what you say. They will do anything to destroy the British."

In June 1780, General Clinton rules that all young men must serve in the British militia. Men with more than four children will guard the towns and farms near their homes. You have to serve. You could join a Loyalist horseback, or cavalry, unit. You're a strong rider. Or you could join the South Carolina Royalists, a special regiment formed by South Carolina men to help the British. As a Royalist, you'll be marching on foot.

To join the Royalists, turn to page **306**.

To join a Loyalist cavalry unit, turn to page **307**.

"Fine, I'll take it to the swamp," you agree. You take the bag of silver and rush out the back door just as the men reach the house. They are British soldiers.

"There!" one of them yells. "He's getting away." They chase after you. They think you are a rebel.

"Shoot him!" someone yells.

Bullets whiz past your head. You toss the silver aside and keep running. You stumble when you reach the swamp. A British soldier aims his musket at your head. "Get up," he commands.

The soldier turns away when someone calls his name. If you move quickly, you may be able to escape.

To follow the soldier's orders, go to page **305**.

To escape, turn to page **317**.

You stand up. The soldier's gun pokes into your back as he leads you back to the house.

Father has returned from town. When he sees you, he roars, "Let my son go! He's no rebel." The soldier lowers his gun.

"You're lucky you weren't shot," Father says after the soldiers leave.

In June 1780, General Clinton orders all young men to serve six months in the British militia. Maybe you'll join the South Carolina Royalists. Loyalist Joseph Robinson formed this group in 1775.

You've also heard of a cavalry regiment forming nearby. This type of regiment fights on horseback. You are an excellent horseman.

To join the South Carolina Royalists, turn to page **306**.

To join the cavalry unit, turn to page **307**.

You join the Royalists and help bring order to Charleston. During the summer of 1780, the British defeat the rebels at the Battle of Camden and the Battle of Fishing Creek. You participate in several raids on rebel farms. Everything goes well until October, when British troops are defeated at the Battle of King's Mountain.

You serve the required six months. You're free to go home. You decide to return to the plantation.

Turn to page **316**.

Small farms dotted the countryside in Lancaster County, South Carolina.

You grew up around horses and are a good rider. Serving with a cavalry regiment uses your skills. You go to Camden, South Carolina. It's under British control. From there you go to Lancaster County, South Carolina. Captain Christian Huck, a Loyalist lawyer from Philadelphia, is your commander. With Huck in charge, you attack a nearby rebel militia camp at Hill's Ironworks. It is an easy victory.

Turn the page.

On July 12, Huck leads your regiment along with a New York mounted regiment and 35 well-trained British soldiers. You go to William Bratton's plantation. Bratton, a rebel leader, isn't home, so you move to nearby Williamson's Plantation. "We'll find oats for the horses there," Huck says. You fall asleep in a field in front of Williamson's house.

You wake to gunfire. Rebels are attacking. You are half-asleep and confused.

"Run!" Huck yells.

To try to get to your horse, turn to page **310**.

To run to the woods, turn to page **312**.

The men knock on the door. "There's no time," you say. "Take this to the attic!" You hand the bag of silver to your sister. She dashes up the stairs.

The soldiers ask for food. Your mother invites them in. Your cook brings them a hearty meal. When they leave, they say they'll be back.

They return the next day. This time, when they leave, they take several horses, a cow, and chickens.

After they leave, Father says, "We must go into hiding before they come again. It won't be pleasant, but we'll be safe. We'll hide in the swamp."

When your family returns a week later, the house has been torn apart. Valuable paintings are slashed, and the cupboards are empty. The horses are gone. You begin repairing the damage.

Turn to page **316**.

Gunfire explodes all around you. Men crumple to the ground. You run to the horses and jump onto the nearest one. "Go!" you yell, slapping it on the rump. The horse bolts forward, taking you to safety. You are lucky. Many Loyalists, including Captain Huck, die at the Battle of Williamson's Plantation.

More defeats follow. In September, your regiment is sent home. There is little hope for a British victory. In October 1781, the final battle of the revolution is fought at Yorktown, Virginia. General Charles Cornwallis, leader of the British forces in the South, surrenders to General George Washington. The war is nearly over, but you are not safe. Loyalists are now threatened by the winning patriots. You must leave South Carolina.

When you arrive home, you find that Mother is eager to leave the war behind. "We have family in Great Britain," she says.

"We'll be safe in East Florida," Father says. "It's a British territory. We'll bring the slaves and begin farming again."

They ask you to help decide.

To go to Great Britain, turn to page **314**.

To go to East Florida, turn to page **315**.

You run for the woods and take shelter. The fighting is over in 10 minutes. When the shooting stops, 35 Loyalists are dead, including Captain Huck. Another 30 are wounded. The rebels disappear as quickly as they arrived. You return to Williamson's Plantation to help the wounded and bury the dead.

The tide has turned against the British. You are with British troops when they are defeated at the Battle of King's Mountain in October 1780. Another defeat comes at the Battle of Cowpens in January 1781. Your regiment heads home, weary and discouraged. In October 1781, the British surrender at the Battle of Yorktown in Virginia.

In 1782 Congress passes a law to seize Loyalist property. Your father's plantation and your uncle's business will be seized. You decide to leave South Carolina.

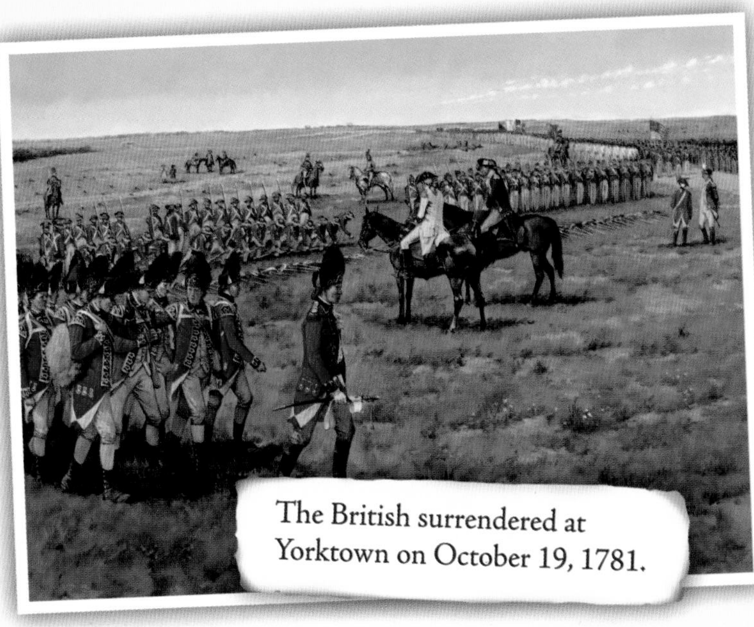

The British surrendered at Yorktown on October 19, 1781.

Many Loyalists are going to Great Britain. "We can start over there," Mother says.

"But if we go to East Florida," Father says, "we can continue farming. I'm a farmer. What would I do in a city? East Florida is a British territory, so we'll be safe there."

To go to Great Britain, turn to page **314**.

To go to East Florida, turn to page **315**.

You go with your family to Great Britain. It should feel like home. But it doesn't. The cities are too big and noisy. You miss country life.

As a reward for your loyal service during the Revolutionary War, the British government gives you land in Nova Scotia. You move to Canada, and your farm prospers. Over time, you become a respected member of the community.

THE END

To follow another path, turn to page 229.
To read the conclusion, turn to page 319.

You go to East Florida. The population of East Florida grows from about 4,000 to more than 17,000 between 1782 and 1783. However, soon after you arrive, you learn that Great Britain has traded East Florida to Spain in exchange for the Bahamas in the western Atlantic Ocean. The British governor, Patrick Tonyn, assures you that the British government will help you move to a new home. In 1784 you move to the capital city of Nassau in the Bahamas. There, you become a successful businessman. You spend the rest of your life in the sunny Bahamas.

THE END

To follow another path, turn to page 229.
To read the conclusion, turn to page 319.

Your father and brother appreciate your help around the plantation. There is a lot of work to do.

One day a group of rebels shows up. They demand money and supplies. "We have nothing left," Father says.

The soldiers are hungry and angry. They strike Father with a musket. He falls to the ground.

"Leave him alone," you yell. "He's an old man."

"You're not," the soldier says, his voice quiet and calm. He points his gun at you and fires. The blast knocks you off your feet. You feel no pain, but you see blood seeping into the dirt. Is it yours? You feel sleepy and strangely peaceful as you shut your eyes for the last time.

THE END

To follow another path, turn to page 229.
To read the conclusion, turn to page 319.

You leap up and knock the soldier's gun aside.

"Stop, or I'll shoot!" he yells.

You know these swamps and woods better than he does. If you can get out of musket range, you'll be safe. You can hide out here for days or even weeks if you have to.

He fires. You feel a burning at your ear. "It's nothing," you say to yourself. You run faster and faster. Then you stumble forward. The bullet has caused bleeding in your brain. You die in a swamp not far from home.

THE END

To follow another path, turn to page 229.
To read the conclusion, turn to page 319.

After the last British soldiers left, George Washington (on white horse) led his troops into New York City on November 25, 1783.

CHAPTER 5

Independence at Last

The American Revolution lasted for eight years. During that time, George Washington often ran out of supplies. But he never ran out of men and women willing to fight for independence. More than 200,000 people, including many women and teenagers, participated in the war. They had the advantage of fighting on land they knew and loved.

British soldiers were fighting 3,000 miles from home. It took weeks to bring men and supplies to the battlefield. Communication with leaders in Great Britain took six weeks to three months. British leaders had to make decisions without knowing whether or not King George would support them.

The first major battle of the war was the Battle of Bunker Hill. General William Howe led 2,400 British troops against 1,500 Americans. The Americans, who had built earthworks at the top of the hill for protection, had the clear advantage. But they eventually ran out of ammunition, and the British won the battle. Despite the victory, the British suffered huge losses. Nearly half the British force was killed or wounded. More British soldiers died at Bunker Hill than in any other single battle of the war.

In 1776 Britain tried to take Charleston, South Carolina. They were soundly defeated. But these early losses did not end the conflict. Britain went on to take control of Boston, New York, and Philadelphia. Even Charleston eventually fell to the British in 1780.

The patriots kept on fighting. They won major victories at Trenton and Princeton, New Jersey, and at Saratoga, New York. The final victory came in Virginia at the Battle of Yorktown in October 1781. When Great Britain's General Cornwallis surrendered at Yorktown, the major fighting stopped. In 1782 Great Britain began withdrawing troops and helping Loyalists leave America.

About one-fifth of the American colonists remained loyal to Great Britain. Loyalists lived in every colony, especially in major cities like Boston, New York, and Philadelphia. Some Loyalists remained in their homes after the war, but many moved to Canada, Great Britain, or East Florida, a British territory.

Benjamin Franklin and John Jay traveled to Paris, France, to work out the terms of the peace treaty. The Treaty of Paris was signed on September 3, 1783. As part of the treaty, Britain gave its territory in East Florida to Spain. Many Loyalists who had settled there moved to British-held islands off the American coast.

Once the war ended, the colonies had to develop a national government. They needed a document to lay out the ideas that would guide the nation. In 1787 the U.S. Constitution was written at a Constitutional Convention in Philadelphia. Convention delegates signed the Constitution on September 17, 1787. It then was sent to the states to be approved. In 1790 Rhode Island became the 13th and final state to approve the U.S. Constitution.

Even before the Constitution was approved, some states demanded changes. Those changes, or amendments, are known as the Bill of Rights. The Declaration of Independence, the Constitution, and the Bill of Rights have guided the United States for more than 200 years.

Timeline

1760 — King George III becomes king of Great Britain.

1765 — British parliament passes the Stamp Act. Colonists protest the taxes.

1768 — British troops arrive in Boston to enforce laws.

1770 — In the Boston Massacre, British troops kill five colonists.

1773 — Patriots dump tea in Boston Harbor.

1774 — The First Continental Congress meets in Philadelphia.

April 1775 — The first shots of the war are fired at Lexington and Concord, Massachusetts.

June 1775 — The British win the Battle of Bunker Hill.

June 1776 — Patriots defeat the British Navy at Sullivan's Island, South Carolina.

July 4, 1776 — Congress ratifies the Declaration of Independence.

September 1777 — Philadelphia falls to the British; Patriots win the Battle of Freeman's Farm at Stillwater, New York.

October 1777 — British General John Burgoyne surrenders at the Battle of Saratoga; the British win the Battle of Germantown, Pennsylvania.

November 1777 — British troops win the Battle of Fort Mifflin.

May 1780 — Charleston, South Carolina, falls to the British.

August 1780 — The British win the Battle of Camden, South Carolina.

October 1780 — Americans win the Battle of King's Mountain, South Carolina.

January 1781 — Americans win the Battle of Cowpens, South Carolina.

October 1781 — British General Cornwallis surrenders at Yorktown, Virginia.

September 3, 1783 — Leaders from Great Britain and the United States sign the Treaty of Paris.

October 1783 — British troops leave New York.

May 1787 — The Constitutional Convention begins in Philadelphia.

1790 — Rhode Island becomes the last state to approve the U.S. Constitution.

Other Paths to Explore

In this book you've seen how the events surrounding the Revolutionary War look different from several points of view.

Perspectives on history are as varied as the people who lived it. You can explore other paths on your own to learn more about what happened. Seeing history from many points of view is an important part of understanding it.

Here are some ideas for other Revolutionary War points of view to explore:

- Many American Indians sided with the British. They feared the American colonists were moving in to claim the land. What would life have been like for an American Indian during the war?

- The British encouraged many southern slaves to join British troops. In exchange, the British promised them freedom after the war. What would fighting on the British side have been like for the slaves?

- The British hired German soldiers, called Hessians, to increase their forces. Most Hessians knew no English. What problems would you have faced as a German fighting on American soil?

Author Biographies

Michael Burgan

Michael Burgan has written numerous books for children and young adults. Many of his books have focused on U.S. history, geography, and the lives of world leaders. Michael has won several awards for his writing, and his graphic novel version of the classic tale *Frankenstein* (Stone Arch Books) was a Junior Library Guild selection.

Elizabeth Raum

Elizabeth Raum has written many nonfiction books for children. She has also written picture books and books for adults. Two of her Capstone You Choose books, *Orphan Trains* (2011) and *Can You Survive Storm Chasing?* (2012), are Junior Library Guild selections.